FISHING FOR
FLUKE

DON KAMIENSKI

FISHING FOR
FLUKE

DON KAMIENSKI

THE FISHERMAN LIBRARY

by Ocean Sport Fishing
1620 Beaver Dam Rd.
Point Pleasant, NJ 08742

Printed in the United States of America

Library of Congress Cataloging-in-Publication Data

ISBN 0-923155-02-3

THE FISHERMAN LIBRARY
Ocean Sport Fishing
1620 Beaver Dam Rd.
Point Pleasant, NJ 08742

Copy Editing . . . . Linda Barrett
Production . . . . Captain Matt Muzslay
Art Direction . . . . Steve and Terri Goione

INTRODUCTION

The fluke, or summer flounder as many people know the species, is one of the Atlantic coast's most popular gamefish. From Massachusetts to Florida there are literally thousands of fishermen who seek this abundant gamefish. And, they don't have to look very far to find good fishing. Most bays, inlets, tidal rivers and coastal areas hold fluke at some time during the year so the fish are an easy mark for all anglers.

Fancy tackle isn't mandatory, nor is a fully rigged and tricked out sportfishing boat. A basic rod and reel and a row boat or small skiff are all that's needed for many anglers to catch uncountable numbers of fluke each season.

But, there is a method to this madness of fluke fishing and like any other type of fishing, there are special places to find them, ideal tackle to help catch more of them and small details required to rig baits and terminal gear that help fool the biggest fluke called doormats because of their huge size. Catching the heavyweight fluke of better than 5 to 6 pounds takes alot of skill and experience.

There's no doubt that simple methods will work, but to be among the elite clan of fluke fishermen who consistently take more fish and larger fish requires extra effort and learning. The best part of learning more about fluke fishing is that you will enjoy catching them even more.

Don Kamienski is one of those gifted fishermen who seem to find fish even on the days when others are having a tough time. Oh sure, Don can have an off day just like the rest of us, but they are infrequent. He's a fanatic about the details of fluke fishing and pays close attention to the underwater structure, the depth, temperature, wind and a host of other variables that make fishing a great success or a disappointing failure.

"Fishing For Fluke" gives you the chance to fish side by side with Don and to share his fluke fishing expertise. You may find some surprises in the book — methods that you may never have thought of before — but there aren't any secrets. The "secrets" of the pro guides and captains is simply taking the time to learn the fish, where it lives and what makes it eat. The best fluke fishermen, like Don, have spent alot of time developing the time tested fishing skills that work day after day. This book brings it all together with easy reading and alot of solid fluke fishing information.

Pete Barrett

ACKNOWLEDGEMENTS

To catch fluke (summer flounder) consistently takes years of practice and first hand knowledge. I'd like to say "Thanks" to the hundreds of avid fluke fishermen, charter and party boat captains, boat livery owners and tackle shop staff who cheerfully and eagerly showed me new and innovative techniques and also some old and nearly forgotten methods that added to my store of fluke fishing knowledge which made my fluke fishing more successful and especially more fun.

Don Kamienski

TABLE
OF
CONTENTS

1
THE FLUKE

Inshore fishermen from Massachusetts to Florida have made the fluke (summer flounder) one of the most sought after gamefish along the Atlantic coast. The ubiquitous fluke is found virtually everywhere including salty rivers and tidal creeks, the wide open bays behind coastal barrier islands and also along the inshore waters from the wash of the surf to deeper waters.

The fluke grows to respectable size and while most fish are in the 2 to 4 pound class, depending on the angler's skill and the season of the year, the chance of hooking a trophy fish is excellent and each year there are many pleasantly surprised fluke fishermen who land a fish of 10 pounds or more. That's a big fluke in anyone's book! The fluke is recognized by the International Game Fish Association as a gamefish and keeps records on the largest fluke caught in various pound test line categories.

Despite the fact that fluke are found in abundance and close to shore, they aren't always so easy to catch. Variables of wind, weather, tides, water temperature and changing seasons sometimes combine to make it difficult to put together a good catch of fish for dinner. This uncertainty adds to the challenge of fluke fishing.

Fluke may be taken by a wide variety of methods from drifting to trolling, baitfishing to casting with artificials — even with a flyrod! It's the skill and knowledge of bait presentation, bottom formations, tides and currents that are prerequisites for successful fluke fishing.

Scientific Classification

The fluke is a member of the flatfish family Bothidae, which includes the winter flounder, halibut, turbot and dab. Its scientific name is *Paralichthys dentatus.* In its southern range below Beach Haven, New Jersey, and on down along the coast to Cape Hatteras it is known locally as summer flounder or, simply, flounder. Northern anglers along New Jersey, the New York Bight, Long Island and up to Massachusetts call it by its more common name of fluke.

Description

The fluke is a left-handed fish, which means that it lies on the bottom on its right side, the eyes and mouth pointing to the left, the abdomen at the lower edge of the body and the tail (or caudal fin) to the right. An easy way of determining if you have a summer flounder as opposed to a winter flounder, is to hold the fish at arm's length with the mouth pointing away from you, and its lower jaw towards the ground. If the pair of eyes and dark side are on the left, you are holding a summer founder or fluke. If the eyes and dark side are on the right, you've caught a winter flounder.

The fluke has a large mouth containing many long, needle-sharp teeth which can easily inflict a nasty cut on a misplaced finger. The shape of the body is narrower than most of the flatfishes. The dorsal fin originates just above and slightly ahead of the eyes and has 85 to 94 soft fin rays, while the anal fin starts behind the ventral fin and has 60 to 73 rays. The shape of the tail (caudal fin) is round when extended, or double-concave when not extended. The right side of the fluke lies on the bottom and is white. The left (or dark) side always faces up.

Both eyes of the adult fluke are on the same side of the head, on the dark side of the fish. But until the larva grows to a length of approximately ½", the eyes are on opposite sides of the head, as normally found on most of the bony fishes. As the larva grows, the right eye begins a migration to the left side of the head. By the time the larva reaches about 1", the right eye has completed its migration, joining the left eye so that both are on the left side of the head. At this point the small fry are very similar in appearance to the adults.

Coloration

The fluke is white on its underside and the top or dark side may be various shades of brown or gray. What they lack in bright coloration is overcome by their ability to quickly move over the bottom and rapidly take on the color of the surrounding sand, mud or gravel by assuming a wide range of tints from almost white through various hues of gray, orange and brown to almost black. Fluke also have the ability to change the color pattern on their bodies to match that of the bottom they are lying on. An ocean floor covered with shells will be imitated with large white splotches. A gravel bottom will be imitated by a mottled body of light and dark spots.

8

Life Stages

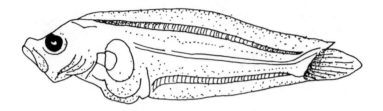

Larva early stage; eyes opposite sides of head.

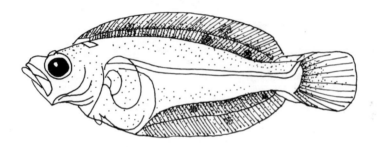

Larva 16mm long; right eye begins migration.

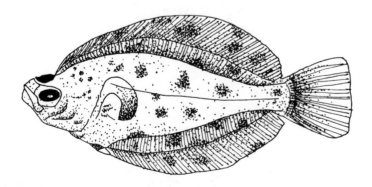

Larva 26mm long; eye migration complete; fry similar in appearance to adult.

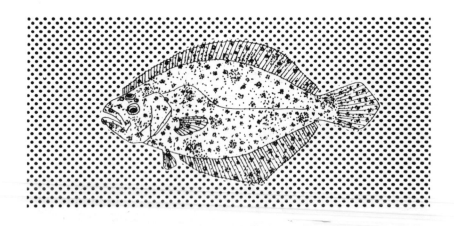

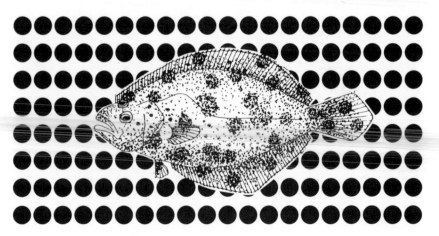

Size Range and Record

The largest fluke ever taken on rod and reel was caught off Chile, South America, and weighed in at 30 pounds, 12 ounces, but the vast majority of fish taken by anglers fall within the one-to three-pound range. A fluke between three and five pounds would be considered a big fish, and any fluke more than six pounds is referred to as a doormat fluke due to its large size. As of the editing of this book, the current world's record fluke is credited to Charlie Nappi, who caught the doormat in 1975 at Montauk, N.Y. It weighed in at 22 pounds, 7 ounces.

While it may be difficult to beat the existing all-tackle record, the International Game Fish Association (IGFA) recognizes the following line classes for fluke: 2; 4; 8; 12; 16; 20; and 30-pound line class. The entries for line class records are divided into a men's class and a women's class. More information about submitting a big fluke catch for a possible record can be obtained by writing: IGFA, 3000 East Las Olas Blvd., Fort Lauderdale, Florida 33316. Additionally, most states along the eastern seaboard keep their own records for fluke, and information regarding these programs can be obtained from the state fish and game departments.

Approximate length-to-weight ratios:

Average Length	Average weight, in pounds
13-14 inches	¾ to 1¼
15-16 inches	1¼ to 2
17-18 inches	2 to 2¾
20 inches	3 to 3½
22 inches	4 to 6
27 inches	7 to 9
30 inches	10 to 14
37 inches	20 plus

Bruce Freeman, New Jersey Marine Fisheries Administrator, checks a fluke for weight, length and takes scale samples for later lab verification of age.

State Laws

Several states have established minimum lengths for a legal fluke. These include: New York (14″), Maryland (12″), Virginia (12″), North Carolina (13″), Delaware (13″), New Jersey (13″). These minimum legal length requirements are strictly enforced with stiff fines imposed on violators. Know and respect the size limits on all fish in your state, not only because it's the law, but also for conservation reasons. The fish are given at least one season to spawn before becoming legal game.

Species Identification

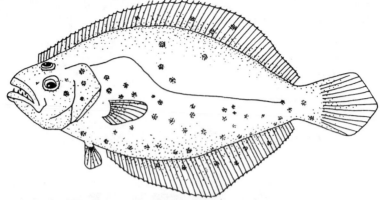

Northern fluke *Paralichthys dentatus.*

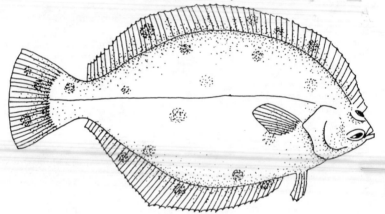

Winter flounder *Pseudopleuronectes americanus.*

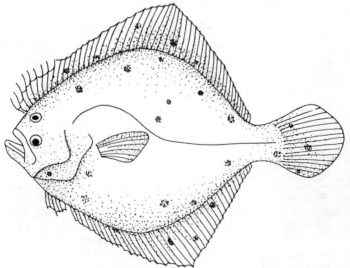

Sundial (Windowpane) *Lophopsetta maculata.*

Identification

Identification of the fluke as a species is quite simple, as there are only two other fish that the angler may confuse it with: the winter flounder and the windowpane, which is more commonly known as a sundial. The accompanying illustration shows a fluke, a winter flounder, and a sundial.

Migration Habits

Fluke are found in great numbers in the inshore waters during the warm summer months. They make their initial appearance in late April. The smaller fish of one to three pounds infiltrate the bays, harbors and estuaries, while the larger fish seem to prefer the deeper ocean waters. Fluke will stay in local haunts with little geographic movement throughout the early summer months. By mid-August the fish begin to move from the bays and harbors to inlets and coastal areas, where they will pause for several weeks to feed heavily in order to fatten up for the fall migration. By the end of September, the bulk of the fluke have started their migration, an offshore movement to the continental shelf, where it is believed the fluke winter until the following March or April, when they begin the inshore movement to inshore waters once again.

As this offshore migration process occurs, spawning takes place. Larvae and post larvae spawned by females four years or older, drift and migrate inshore and enter the coastal nursery areas of North Carolina, Chesapeake Bay, and the eastern shore of Virginia from October to May. Juvenile fluke will remain in these inshore waters for their first year, and then join the offshore migration as two-year-olds.

Shoal waters like those shown at this coastal inlet are favorite haunts of the summer flounder and place the fish within easy reach of fishermen.

Fluke, also known as summer flounder, are every man's inshore gamefish and are among the most popular of the inshore species caught by recreational anglers.

Feeding Habits

Fluke spend most of their lives on or near the bottom. During their summer stay in inshore waters, fluke prefer a sandy bottom in which they can bury themselves with only their eyes protruding. Fluke also like a gravel bottom they can blend with by changing the texture of their body pattern, and will often lie motionless for long periods of time while camouflaged. But they are capable of surprising bursts of speed and will quickly pounce on any unwary prey that ventures within striking range. Fluke are also fond of lurking in eel grass in shallow water, or among the pilings of docks.

The fluke is a predacious fish, feeding on almost any smaller bait they can capture — squid, shrimp, killifish, sand eels, spearing, menhaden, herring, mullet, etc. They are fierce and active in their pursuit of prey, often chasing schools of small baitfish right up to the surface. The fluke is one of the most active members of the flatfish family, unlike its sluggish cousin, the winter flounder.

The fluke employs two methods of feeding: from ambush and by pursuit. They will strike from ambush by camouflaging their bodies to blend in with the surrounding bottom conditions as previously described. They will also feed by chasing prey, but are at a disadvantage because they are only capable of short bursts of speed. Therefore, fluke will seek out bottom formations that create water turbulence which tends to put baitfish at a disadvantage, putting the fluke on an even footing with their prey.

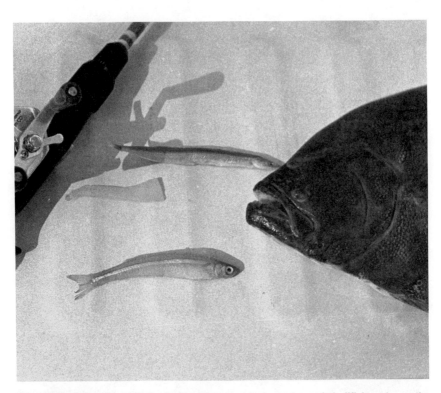

If it swims, fluke will eat it! Squid, spearing, sandeels, crabs and shellfish make up the bulk of the diet of the summer flounder.

2
TACKLE

The most common mistake made by would-be fluke fishermen is to fish with tackle that is too heavy for the game — rabbit hunting with an elephant gun, so to speak. It would be bad enough if the only negative result of using a "broom handle and winch" for fluke was to take the sport out of the battle, but there is an additional consequence: you won't take many fluke on heavy tackle. Don't make the mistake of believing that your trusty codfishing outfit is also "good enough" for taking fluke — it isn't.

When chosing a rod and reel combination for fluke fishing, four factors must be taken into consideration: how a fluke takes a bait; how they fight; where the fishing is going to be done; and by what method. The ideal fluke outfit should possess three qualities: minimal weight; moderate backbone; and finally, maximum sensitivity.

Today's fluke angler has a remarkable array of excellent tackle available. From spinning to conventional there are new light weight rods and reels that offer superior "feel", durability and sensitivity that was only dreamed of a decade ago. If you aren't sure what tackle is best in your fishing area, I suggest you consult with one or more proprietors of local tackle shops. They often know what the local "hot shots" are using and can recommend ideal tackle that will match the average size of the fish, the type of fishing and your own angling skills and pocketbook.

Rods

How fluke take a bait and fight largely determines what type of rod blank is preferred. Fluke have a habit of picking up bait very softly and holding it in their mouths. If they feel no resistance and think the bait isn't capable of escaping, the fluke will then begin to swallow it. But, if resistance is felt, they will just hold onto the bait or drop it entirely, so it is extremely important that the angler be able to detect this soft pick up of the fish so that he can "drop-back" the bait so no resistance will be felt by the fluke. Short, stiff rods just aren't capable of detecting this soft touch. As a result, anglers using such rods usually don't even realize that they are getting a bite. A rod with a light tip that will register the slightest tap or change in the line tension or movement is an absolute must.

While fiberglass rods are usually adequate for fluke fishing, the use of a graphite rod is a distinct advantage. This type of rod material telegraphs what is happening to the bait to a greater degree to the angler's hand. The increased feel and sensitivity of graphite for detecting fluke cannot be overemphasized.

Once fluke have been hooked, they try to hug the bottom so, in addition to a rod having a sensitive tip to feel fluke, it must have enough backbone in the butt section to bring the fluke off the bottom and to a waiting net.

Line Selection

By far, the vast majority of fluke anglers use premium monofilament line in the 8-20-pound class. For tidal rivers, back bays and harbor fishing, line testing out at 8-12 lbs. is ideal since the waters of these areas are fairly shallow, and the fluke are usually smaller. An additional benefit of using the lighter lines is that they require less sinker weight to keep the bait near the bottom because the smaller line diameter has less water drag. When fishing offshore lumps or places that contain rocky bottoms, the use of line in the 17-20-pound class is suggested. There are a number of talented fluke anglers that have switched over to dacron line which has less stretch for increased "feel" of the fish, and quicker hook-setting capabilities.

Sunlight is the worst enemy of monofilament lines, and therefore your gear should be stored in a cool, dark and dry place instead of the rear window of a pickup truck. It's even a good idea to strip off 10 feet of line before each trip because this length of line takes most of the abuse from fish or fisherman. If you do a lot of fluke fishing during the year, it's also a good idea to replace the line on the reel before the first trip in the spring. Rather than replacing the entire spool of line, only replace the first 100 yards as this section, if frayed, might cost you a big fish someday.

Spinning Tackle

Spinning gear is perhaps the most popular type of tackle for catching fluke because it can be used from small private boats, party boats, beaches, piers, jetties, bulkheads and where casting is sometimes essential. However, all spinning tackle is not the same. The equipment used in bays, tidal rivers and harbors tends to be smaller and lighter than that used in offshore or deep coastal waters. A good rod and reel combination to use for shallow water fluke fishing is a six-foot, heavy-action, freshwater or light salt water outfit. This type outfit has plenty of guts to land 1-to 3-pound fish; and a fluke over five

Spinning tackle is preferred by many fluke specialists because it is so easy to use, especially when casting small lures or bait.

pounds will provide an exciting few minutes. Quality spinning reels filled with 8-12-pound test line are some excellent choices for fluke fishing.

When using spinning gear from either a land-based position or from a party boat, tackle that is slightly longer and heavier is recommended. Since casting and retreiving a weighted bait is necessary in this type of fishing, a 7 - 8 foot rod with a light tip but sturdy butt section is suggested. My own choice is an eight-foot graphite rod and a medium sized spinning reel. With this combination, I can flip my bait away from the other party boat anglers or to a pocket of fluke that may be residing off the tip of a jetty or downtide of a bulkhead or pier. Most talented fluke anglers who use spinning gear while either drifting or trolling, will fish with the bail open and with the index finger holding the line. When the angler feels the fish mouthing the bait, it's just a matter of lifting his finger and allowing the line and bait to drop back to the hungry fluke. Turn the handle to automatically close the bail, and then set the hook.

Conventional tackle takes an "educated thumb" to avoid backlashes while casting, but the latest model levelwinds are perfect for fluke fishing.

Baitcasting and Tackle

Baitcasting tackle is probably the most versatile type of equipment for fluke fishing. With this gear, you can drift, troll, cast, and even jig bucktails for fluke. Anglers armed with a 5½-6-foot lightweight graphite, one handed casting rod with a heavy action can really put a dent in the local fluke population. A rod like this gives great sensitivity with the slightest tap or softest pick-up of a fish quickly transmitted to the angler's fingertips. Because a graphite casting outfit tends to be light in weight, many anglers fish with two rods at the same time without feeling any undue fatique.

While a sensitive casting rod is certainly a plus, more important is a reel that is matched to the rod. Each year the quality reel manufacturers such as Shimano, Daiwa, Penn, Garcia, Ryobl and Shakespeare enhance their line of casting reels to help control backlashes, to provide for easier casting, and to stand up longer to the corrosive elements associated with saltwater fishing. The Penn 940, the Shimano Bantam series, the Daiwa PMF group, and Garcia Ambassadeurs, are all excellent choices in a baitcasting reel. It's doubtful that you'll need to equip these reels with more than 12-17-pound test line, as there isn't a fluke swimming that can break these line classes if the drag is properly set on the reel. A good rule of thumb is to set any drag at one-third the breaking strength of the line. As our spinning friends fished with an open bail to allow for a drop-back of a bait to a hungry fluke, those using casting equipment tend to use their reels in free spool, lifting their thumb off the spool when a fish is felt, allowing the line to feed off the reel.

One advantage of conventional tackle is the added "feeling" since line can be in direct contact with the angler's fingers to feel the lightest hit.

Conventional Tackle

Here again, depending on the water depth, or the bottom features you're encountering, you can employ various types of conventional gear. For thin water fishing, a Penn 9MS level wind reel or a Daiwa Sealine 27H reel on a six-foot fast taper rod is suggested, but if you plan to be fishing in waters over 40 feet, a medium or heavy action rod with a medium taper is our choice. For deep offshore fluking, a Penn Squidder with a Shakespeare Ugly Stick rod are both excellent choices. Let me pause here and say that buying a rod and reel is like picking out a necktie or betting on a horse. Everybody has their own preference as to what is the right outfit for them. The tackle suggested in this reference book should only be used as a starting point in that it has proven to be effective for fluke fishing. When you actually put cold cash on the counter for a new rod and reel, make sure it fits your fishing style and needs.

Heavier conventional tackle is only used in deep water fishing for fluke where heavier sinkers are needed to take baits to the bottom.

Few fluke fishermen try their hand at fly fishing for their favorite gamefish but a properly presented streamer can be very effective in shallow water.

Flycasting

Fluke are at times an easy mark for the fly-rodder, especially when they are feeding in shallow bays or shoal waters adjacent to sand bars. Rods 8½-to 9-feet which are able to push a WF8 or WF9 line are required. Sinking tip lines work best in bay areas, and a sinking line is required when fishing in the deeper channels. A few inches of strip lead on the leader will also help in sinking the fly. The Shakespeare Medalist and other quality reels by Garcia and Martin are good choices for this kind of fly fishing.

Fly patterns are usually very bright with lots of tinsel, yellows, white, pinks and reds. The Joe Brooks Blonde Streamer series, Lefty's Deceiver, Lyman's Terror and Gibb's Striper Fly are typical of the patterns effective for fluke. Shrimp patterns such as the Boyle Shrimp, Pink Shrimp and Kukonen Shrimp are also deadly, but just about any pattern that imitates a small baitfish or crab will take fluke at times.

3
EQUIPMENT

In addition to using a balanced rod and reel combination, there are certain pieces of equipment that should accompany a fluke angler on his fishing trips. However, depending on whether the angler is either landbased or fishing from a boat, the equipment needed tends to be different. This chapter will cover some suggested equipment categories.

While it's true that fluke accessory gear can be kept very simple, the best fluke anglers rely on specialized equipment to help catch bait, keep the baits alive in between fishing trips, store rigs and lures, help with filleting the catch and in general make fishing easier and more productive.

One of the big breakthroughs in the last few years has been the greater reliance by flukers on graph recorders to show the changing bottom contours. Newer innovations include the use of video scopes and LCD dot matrix type "recorders" which are a cross between a paper graph and a flasher. The investment in any one of these bottom reading electronics marvels will add many fish to your yearly total of fluke.

Even Loran C receivers, once the exclusive toys of offshore tuna anglers, are now used extensively by fluke fishermen to repeatedly get back on highly productive fishing areas. The cost of Loran has dropped from the $2000 range dwon to new compact units that are one quarter of that price.

Of particular interest to any fisherman is a daily log book. Our memory often fades in only a few days and a written record that describes a good fishing spot and a special bait rigging method can never be forgotten once written down in a log book.

Depth Recorders

For the boat angler, one of the most important pieces of equipment that can help provide a successful day of fluke fishing is a good depth recorder. The advantage of using a recorder is not just its ability to tell you the water depth, but it shows how the bottom structure changes. You could be on the edge of a channel; over an underwater hump; on the border of a tidal pool; or on the slope of a sand bar knowing that fluke like these changes in the bottom's contour. Using a depth recorder will help pinpoint these structure breaks, and subsequently get you more fish.

For a starting unit, a flasher-type recorder that provides both a shallow water range and a moderate water depth range is ideal. Recorders manufactured by Si-Tex, Lowrance, and Humminbird are but three quality recorders on the market. I should point out that any recorder is only as good as the quality of installation performed on the unit, so follow the instructions regarding installation for the best possible results.

Once you feel comfortable with a flashing recorder, you may want to graduate to a graph paper recorder where the variation in bottom structure or contour is etched on a moving piece of paper by a stylus. The advantage of using a paper recorder over a flashing type of recorder is threefold. First, with the paper recorder you have a permanent record of the bottom's contour which can be analyzed during a post-fishing trip evaluation to see why you caught fluke in one location and not in another. Secondly, you needn't be watching the recorder to detect changes in the bottom. Thirdly, the paper graph recorders tend to be somewhat easier to interpret when you are viewing the bottom variations. The Lowrance, Si-Tex and the Humminbird are excellent examples of quality graph recorders. Graph recorders are somewhat more expensive than the flashing units, but they are certainly worth the price difference.

Today's up-to-date fluke fishermen uses graph recorder, LCD depth meter, Loran and CB or VHF radio to help pinpoint good fishing.

Landing Net

A large net is probably the most critical piece of equipment to have when fishing for fluke. While it is often unnecessary to net small fish, fluke of three pounds and above should *ALWAYS* be netted to be on the safe side. Even though you may be able to look down in the water and see that the fish has the hook entirely in its mouth, this does not necessarily mean that the hook has been firmly embedded. The roof of a fluke's mouth is very hard and difficult to penetrate, and the hook will often just grab the loose flesh inside. While this is usually firm enough to bring the fish to the boat, the flesh will often tear and free the hook if a large fluke is simply lifted over the gunwale. In addition, fluke shake like crazy when lifted out of the water.

The net should have a diameter of between 18 and 30 inches. The handle should be as long as possible without becoming awkward to use or store in your boat. If you own a small skiff and storage space is at a minimum, you can buy a net with a collapsible handle to make the net more compact when not in use. Net handles are usually either made of wood or aluminum. Aluminum handles are preferred for two reasons: they are lighter and easier to handle in a strong current, and they float on the surface, making it a simple chore to spot and pick one up if accidentally dropped in the water. If your landing net is several years old, it's a good idea to check the netting for rotted or frayed sections. Should this be the case, replace the net as you don't want a large fluke dropping out the bottom of your weakened net.

A high quality, wide mouthed landing net is an essential part of the summer flounder angler's tackle.

Hook Disgorger

It is not unusual to hook a fluke in the gills or deep down in the mouth because of the manner in which they take a bait. Fluke have needle-sharp teeth and narrow mouths, making it awkward and inadvisable to put one's finger down the gullet in order to remove a hook. At these times a hook disgorger is a valuable aid to the angler. They are inexpensive and may be purchased at almost any bait and tackle store. The mechanical hook disgorger is used by grasping the bend of the hook in the plier-like jaws and twisting and pushing until the hook is freed. A simple hook disgorger can be made at home by simply making a V-shape notch in the end of a wooden dowel or metal rod. The "V" of the shaft is placed over the bend of the hook and pushed downwards, removing the hook from the flesh with a backwards movement.

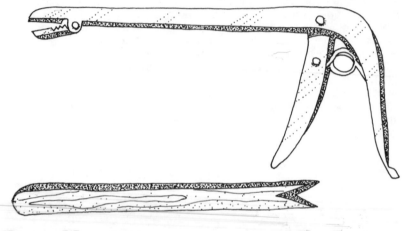

Tape Measure

A plastic tape measure like those normally used in sewing is inexpensive and may be rolled up neatly and stored in the tackle box. Or the angler can attach a yardstick somewhere in the interior of his skiff where it will be easily accessible. You can also paint a mark on your rod or even a boat seat to show minimum legal length for fluke in your home waters.

Fluker's Fish Box

The containers fluke anglers use to store their catch will determine the condition of the meat when it is time to clean and cook the fish. Those anglers that stuff their catch into a five-gallon bucket or into a plastic bag on a hot summer day will invariably have a pile of soft-flesh fluke on their hands at the end of a trip, which not only makes cleaning difficult, but also causes the meat to be less than appetizing. If space is available on your boat or shore-based position, I'd suggest that you store all fluke in a well-insulated cooler. A recommended minimal size for such a fluke box is 48 quarts, while the upper size range can be as large as 86 quarts, which is especially nice for you optimistic fluke anglers!

Rather than placing the fluke in the cooler with a few ice cubes to keep them fresh, I'd suggest the following: As you begin catching fluke, place them into a cooler that contains a 10-pound *BLOCK* of ice. Next, add a quantity of salt water to the cooler that just covers the fish. The block of ice will chill the salt water, which, in turn, will chill the fluke. As more fish are added to the cooler, you may have to increase the water supply, but the combination of the salt water and ice will accomplish two things. First, it will keep your fluke's meat very fresh, and secondly it will keep the flesh firm. This freshness and firmness of the meat will not only make the cleaning of the fluke an easier chore, but also the eating of the fish a more enjoyable experience.

Fish Stringer

A plastic or metal fish stringer is always a handy item to have when fishing for fluke from a skiff, pier or the beach. The fluke are put on a stringer as soon as they have been caught, then placed back in the water. This will keep the fish alive indefinitely; assuring a fresh catch for the dinner table.

Caution should be taken when using a fish stringer from a skiff. The string of fish must be removed from the water whenever the engine is started and the boat put into motion, or it may become fouled in the propeller, or fish may be ripped off from being pulled rapidly through the water. It's even a good idea to attach the end of your stringer to the outboard motor handle or near the ignition switch to remind you that there's a stringer of fluke that needs attention. A line usually must be attached to the stringer when being used from a pier so that it can reach the water. A longer line is necessary for beach fishing so that the fish can be kept in the water while the line is secured to a sand spike or other stationary object.

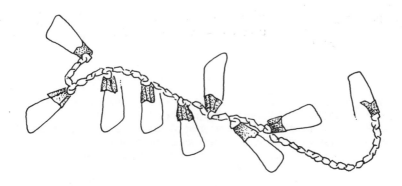

Marker Buoy

Marker buoys are used to mark a bottom formation that has been located or an area where a fluke has been caught, allowing the angler to return repeatedly to the exact spot on subsequent drifts. They may be made easily and cheaply at home — all that is needed is material for a float, line and weight. The best thing to use for a float is a one-gallon antifreeze container because they are usually either a bright yellow or red plastic, colors that are easily spotted on a wide expanse of water. Gallon-size bleach bottles may also be used, but their white color makes them almost impossible to see if there is any white water, a definite disadvantage. Colored blocks of styrofoam can be purchased at most marinas and can be cut up to make excellent buoy floats.

Just about anything can be used for the line connecting the float to the weight. Old monofilament line, cord, clothesline rope, etc. Keep in mind that you may lose a buoy, so make them as inexpensively as possible to keep your monetary losses to a minimum. For shallow water fishing in the bays and inshore waters, 25 feet of line should be used. For deep water ocean and wreck fishing, 100 to 150 feet of line is. necessary. Wrap the line around the buoy float and secure it with a strip of masking tape or electrical tape to prevent the coils of line from springing off and tangling up. When the buoy is to be used, simply remove the tape and throw the buoy into the water. Remember to toss the buoy when you *hook* the fish, not when you *land* it. The distance between the hooking location and the landing spot can often be several hundred feet apart. Obviously, you want to be able to duplicate the productive drift through the hotspot by starting up-current from where the fish was hooked.

The weight that is used to anchor the marker buoy should also be the most inexpensive item at your disposal. Old sash weights, scrap iron, auto engine parts, sinkers or even a brick will work. It is important that the weight is heavy enough to prevent the marker buoy from "walking" along the bottom. This occurs when the action of the waves lifts the buoy, which then exerts a pulling force on the line that will lift the weight off the bottom, moving it slightly. Even if the weight only moved an inch with each wave, it would only be a short time before the buoy has "walked" a considerable distance from its initial position, which can often be extremely critical.

Live Bait Car

A bait car (sometimes known as a killie car) is a container made of wood and wire mesh screening that is used to transport live killies and other baitfish for a day's fishing. The bait car is kept over the side on a line while the boat is not under power, keeping the bait alive. Individual baitfish are removed through a trap door in the top of the car. This is a very simple and effective method of keeping baitfish lively, and bait cars are relatively inexpensive (as opposed to aerator set ups) and are available at almost any bait and tackle outlet. The handy man can easily fashion his own from scraps of wood and a square foot of old screen. The drawbacks of using a bait car are twofold: if the angler is forgetful and doesn't bring the car into the boat when he is going to move to a new location, it is very possible to injure and even drown the baitfish as the water rushes into the bait car as the boat moves. Also, keeping the bait car out of the water during long runs can be harmful to the killies. A better way to store live killies is to place some ice cubes on the bottom of a small cooler. On top of the cubes, place a small board that is covered with a wet towel. The killies can then be placed on this wet cloth. Add no water to the cooler but cover it to protect the bait from the sun's heat. The moisture and coolness from the ice will keep most of your bait fresh and alive even on the hottest days.

Bait Traps

Live or fresh-dead bait should be used for fluke whenever possible. Unfortunately, the only baitfish that can be purchased live is the killiefish, and even they are in short supply on occasion. Spearing (a.k.a. silversides) and sand eels (a.k.a. sand launce) can only be purchased frozen and are virtually never available in live or fresh-dead forms. When fresh, the flesh of both the spearing and the sand eel is very firm and stays on a hook well. But the freezing process breaks the flesh down, rendering it soft and mushy and difficult to

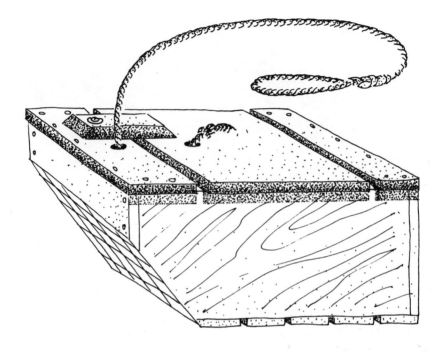

keep on a hook. Both baitfish are excellent fluke baits when fresh, but somewhat less effective when frozen, so it's a good idea for the angler to provide his own supply of fresh bait whenever possible. This is best accomplished with the use of a seine, umbrella net or bait trap.

SEINE. A seine can range in size from 10 to 30 feet in length and two to four feet in depth with floats running along the top and weights spaced along the bottom to hold the seine vertical. A large supply of baitfish can be obtained in a very short period of time with a seine, but two people must enter the water in order to do so. The seine is carried into the water and stretched parallel with the beach. They slowly walk towards the beach, forming a pocket with the seine that captures any baitfish swimming between them and the beach.

UMBRELLA NET. A simpler method of acquiring a supply of baitfish is by using an umbrella net, which requires only one person to operate. This is simply a three- or four-foot-square piece of netting stretched between a stiff wire frame with a line attached to the center. Bread crumbs, canned mackerel or cat food is placed in the center of the net and it is lowered two to three feet into the water from a dock or bulkhead. The net is held motionless until a quantity of baitfish can be observed swimming over the net to get at the food. The net is then quickly jerked up on the dock, hopefully with a large number of baitfish inside. This method is very simple and a good day's supply of fresh baitfish can be quickly obtained. The umbrella also folds into a cylinder shape for convenient storage between uses.

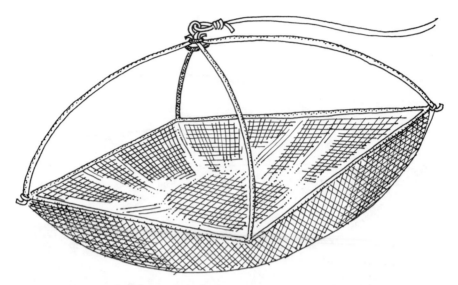

BAIT TRAP. This method of obtaining fresh bait requires little effort on the part of the angler. The wire mesh bait trap is baited and lowered over the side of a boat at dockside and left to do the work of capturing baitfish while the angler is absent. The trap uses the same principle as the lobster pot — each end of the trap has an inverted cone-shaped passage, allowing the baitfish to easily swim into the trap in search of food. Once inside the trap, however, the baitfish must find the small opening, only slightly larger than its body, to get out. This is difficult, and the baitfish will not make too great an effort to escape from the trap because there is an ample food supply and it is safe from the jaws of predators.

The bait trap will catch sand eels, spearing, small eels, killies, bergalls and an assortment of small crabs that can be used as bait for species other than fluke. It's a good practice to keep a bait trap in the water where your boat is docked. Bait that is left over at the end of the day's fishing can be put in the trap to attract the baitfish to be used on the next fishing venture.

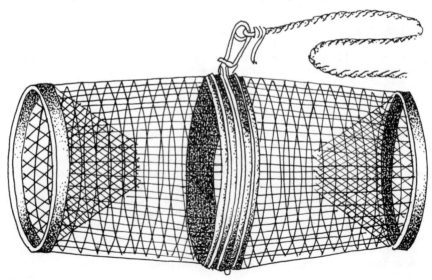

Chum Pot

A chum pot can be invaluable when the fluke are spread over a wide area and it becomes necessary to attract them to the boat. Wire-mesh chum pots come in various sizes and may be purchased at almost any bait and tackle shop and can be used for other species of fish such as flounder, porgies, seabass and striped bass. A plastic-meshed onion or orange bag can also be used effectively by simply adding a few rocks or bricks for weight to take it to the bottom.

A variety of chum can be used in a chum pot to attract foraging fluke to your baited lines. Ground-up mossbunker (menhaden) is always in good supply, or you can make your own chum by putting some of those mackerel caught in the spring through the meat grinder and freezing the chum in wax milk cartons for later use.

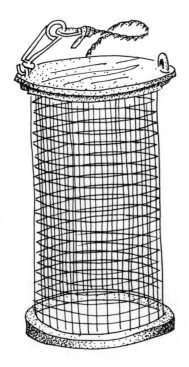

Fillet Knife

A good fillet knife should always be on hand for cutting strip baits from fluke, sand sharks, sea robins or mackerel and to fillet the catch at the end of the day. The knife should have a thin but stiff blade and be kept razorsharp. Use a sharpening tool like Cutmaster made by Bear Archery Company. It was originally designed for the sharpening of broadheads on hunting arrows, but makes an excellent sharpening tool that costs just a few dollars, and can be easily fit into a tackle box or spare jacket pocket. A few brief strokes with the Cutmaster along the blade will turn a dull knife into an effective filleting tool. It's even a good idea to bolt a knife sharpener to your cleaning board.

Author's wife, Helen, uses a stringer to help keep fish fresh until ready to be filleted for dinner.

34

Log Book

One of the "secrets" of successful fluke fishing is the ability to collect, record and evaluate the tremendous amount of information concerning wind speed, wind direction, baitfish supplies and tidal currents that will affect each area's fluke productivity. By noting these variables in a log book or fishing diary over a period of time, it is possible to analyze the information and discover definite feeding patterns of fluke under various conditions to successfully predict where the fish will be feeding. This saves valuable fishing time that would otherwise be spent trying to locate fish. As much information as possible should be gathered and written down in a log that is kept exclusively for fluke fishing. Among the important pieces of information that should be entered in a log are:

Date _____
Location of trip _____
Water temperature _____
Wind direction _____
Wind speed _____
Wind clarity _____
Stage of tide _____
Baitfish in water _____
Stomach contents of fluke caught _____
Type of bait used _____
Type of artificials used (incl. color) _____
How fish took bait _____
Fishing techniques used (drifting, trolling, chumming, bucktailing) _____
Total number of fluke caught _____
Distribution of the number caught by location and fishing technique _____
Type of bottom _____
Fishing companions _____
Other species caught _____
Comments _____

It is often impractical to stop while fishing in order to make entries in a log, so information should be written down as soon as possible after a fishing trip while it is fresh in your mind. It's also a good idea to make a few sketches of the most productive area.

Tackle Boxes

Regardless of where you fish for fluke, you need something to carry hooks, leaders, sinkers, swivels and a host of other essential pieces of gear. While there are many tackle containers on the market today, I tend to favor those boxes that provide you with the capability to re-arrange the sections within the tackle box as my fishing requirements change. If you want longer compartments in which to store leader material and filleting knives, or if you want shorter compartments in which to store bucktails or hooks, look for a box like the Plano Magnum style. This type of box can allow for up to 62 compartments of various sizes and has space for both extra reel storage and artificial baits. The acrylic "see-through" lid allows immediate location of all gear and protects the tackle from harmful sunlight.

Many boats have built-in live wells that are perfect for keeping a catch of fluke alive and in good condition so they don't spoil.

Nets with handles about 6 feet long are helpful when fishing in a small skiff.

Miscellaneous Equipment Items

Unless you have a phenomenal streak of good luck, there are a few items of comfort you should take fluke fishing. The first item on the list is a good set of foul weather gear. No matter what the weatherman says on Friday night, you can expect him to be wrong some percentage of the time on Saturday morning when you're on the water trying for fluke. While some people prefer to wear the poncho type of protection, I like the two-piece outfit with pants and jacket made of a heavy rubber fabric. Wearing just the bottoms on a cool spring or fall morning not only provides some additional warmth, but also a handy place to wipe your fish-stained hands instead of on your clean pants. Some anglers carry a hand towel for this purpose.

If you fish the back-bay marsh areas of the coastline, you will invariably come under the attack of green-head flies, gnats, and mosquitos. Some anglers and commercial clammers swear by the use of Avon bath oil (Skin-So-Soft) to fend off annoying flying insects. Having used the product for the past two seasons, I can personally attest to its effectiveness.

Other items that can be brought along include a pair of polaroid sunglasses, a screwdriver and seasick pills.

Finally, if you fish for fluke mainly from the stone jetties that dot our coastline, I'm sure that you've encountered rock areas that were extremely slippery due to a combination of sea growth and salt water. To prevent an untimely spill resulting in possible serious injury, wear a pair of golf rubbers which contain steel spikes through the heel and sole areas. The advantage of using cleated rubbers is that they can be slipped on over sneakers, hip boots, waders and knee boots with minimal effort, and the spikes can be replaced when they wear out. These rubbers can be purchased at many tackle stores and sport shops. Similar rubbers can also be obtained by contacting: Walt's Walkers, P.O. Box 32, Manahawkin, N.J. 08050.

4
RIGGING UP

Rigging for fluke is quite simple and contrary to the opinions held by some anglers, you don't need alot of fancy terminal gear like spinners and glittering pearl beads to fool these bottom hugging fish. While there are a number of fluke fishermen who still use these added attractors on their rigs, most flukers believe the rigs are more effective when things are kept to the basics.

Just about any rig you will tie will do the job of catching fluke so long as it performs two functions. It must present the bait in a naturall, life-like manner and the rig must also be designed so it will avoid getting tangled or fouled on the bottom.

The vast majority of the time, fluke fishing is done while drifting or by trolling. The wrong choice of a sinker or improperly tied leader can get hung up on a bottom obstruction as the boat moves along. The result with a poorly tied rig is a snapped line, perhaps even losing the entire rig. A better selection of a sinker and properly tied leader will allow the rig to bounce over these obstructions saving you not only lost rigs but also wasted fishing time.

Top notch fluke anglers keep their rigs pre-tied and ready for immediate use so when a rig is lost, they can be back in action right away with no lost time fumbling to tie up a new hook and leader.

The best fluke fishermen are also inventive and frequently change small details in the rig to accommodate changing fishing conditions. A longer drop down from the leader to the sinker is one trick used by party boat and deep water fluke anglers when the speed of the drift increases as wind or current moves the boat faster. Slow drift speeds allow a shorter drop down to the sinker.

Choose the rig carefully, use only the best quality hooks, snaps, swivels and leader material, and you'll enjoy your fishing much more.

Tying Your Own Rigs

The angler can save a considerable amount of money and receive much self-satisfaction by tying his own fluke rigs. All that is necessary is a quantity of the materials listed below and a little patience until you master the four basic knots that are sufficient to tie any bottom rig. It's a good idea to make up a quantity of fluke rigs at home during your spare time.

Materials

All the materials necessary for tying fluke rigs are usually available for purchase at the better-stocked bait and tackle outlets. Purchase them in quantity whenever possible to save money.

HOOKS. There are several styles of excellent fluke hooks such as the Ryder, Pacific Bass, Claw or Beak type, and especially popular in recent years is the English style wide bend. Many fluke fishermen favor this last hook because of its wide gap design which, they feel, results in more hookups. Fluke are not hook-shy, so when in doubt as to the size, favor the larger choice. When fluke are in the 1 - 3-pound range, use 2/0 or 3/0 hooks, and use 4/0 to 5/0 when the fluke are in the 4 - 8-pound class. Purchase your hooks unsnelled in boxes of 100. Split them with a buddy and half the cost.

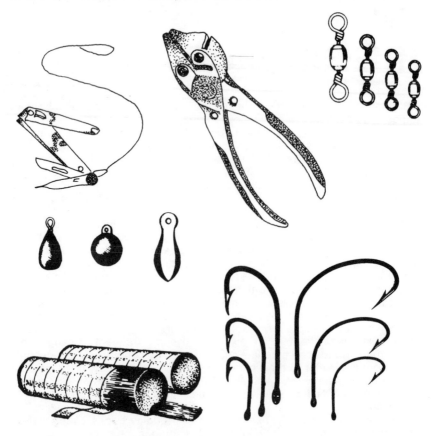

Empty 35mm film canisters are excellent storage containers for loose hooks. Be sure to mark the top of the canister, using a waterproof felt tip pen, with the size of hook. After running several controlled tests in which different-colored hooks were used, we've found that for some reason, the fluke were attracted to the gold color hook more so than they were to silver- or black-colored hooks. So, keep this color preference in mind when selecting hooks. Also, there is no such thing as a lucky hook from a previous trip, so always use sharpened new hooks. Remember that it isn't that $50-reel or that $30-rod that first comes in contact with the fluke . . . it's that 3¢-hook!

LEADER MATERIAL. Nylon leader material is not the same as the monofilament line that is loaded on a reel. It is harder and has a large diameter which is excellent for rig-making because the knots will not unravel as easily. It is also stiffer, so the rig and snell will not tangle. It may be purchased in 30-foot coils or in pre-cut 36-inch strands. Twenty to 30-lb. test leader is ideal for making fluke rigs.

BARREL SWIVELS. The only piece of hardware necessary for a fluke rig is a 1/0 barrel swivel to prevent excessive line twist. All other connecting links may be made with knots. Purchase black swivels whenever possible rather than shiny stainless steel or brass swivels. Bluefish are often found feeding in the same area as fluke and it is not uncommon for a blue to eat a shiny swivel, cutting the line with its sharp teeth and severing the rig. A barrel swivel also acts as a sinker-stop on the fish-finder rig.

FISHERMAN'S PLIERS. A handy aid to have when tying rigs is a pair of fisherman's pliers. They may be used to grasp a hook, cut the line or hold one end of the line when tightening a knot to prevent the line from cutting your hands. Pliers may be purchased with a sheath and carried on your belt while fishing.

ANGLER'S CLIP. Actually a fingernail clipper, they are excellent for trimming knots without putting the unwanted nicks in the line that are often made accidentally when using a relatively cumbersome knife. Clippers are inexpensive and easily carried in the tackle box.

HOOK HONE. A hook hone is used to sharpen the points of hooks, which often come from the factory somewhat dull. All hooks should be sharpened to a needle-point and kept that way. A hone can be an abrasive stone or a file. The latter does a quicker job of sharpening.

SINKERS. The bank, flat, dipsey and ball sinker patterns are preferred for fluke fishing because their rounded shapes allow them to roll over bottom obstructions without hanging up. Carry a full range of sizes and use the lightest weight necessary to hold the rig on the bottom.

Knots

There are several basic knots to know in order to tie almost any bottom rig, and they are easily mastered with a little practice and patience.

There are, however, a few tricks to knot tying that you should know to make things easier. Before tightening a knot, wet it with saliva for lubrication. This will allow the knot to tighten up evenly, preventing any binding. It's also important that the knot is tightened *SLOWLY* by evenly pulling two ends in opposite directions. Don't try to tighten a knot with quick, jerky movements or it will bind incorrectly. Clip the excess line protruding from a knot no shorter than an eighth of an inch to prevent it from unraveling.

Improved clinch knot

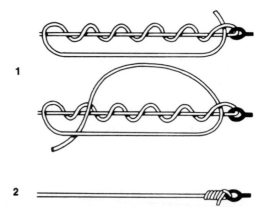

An old standby, this is a basic knot for attaching hooks, lures and swivels. It works best with monofilament lines up to 20-pound-test.

1. Pass the line through the eye of the hook, lure or swivel. Double back and make five turns around the standing line. Hold the coils, pass the tag end through the first opening behind the eye, then through the big loop as shown.
2. Hold the standing line and the free end and pull the coils tight. Make sure the coils are next to each other, not crossed over. Slide the knot against the eye and clip the tag end.

Surgeon's end loop

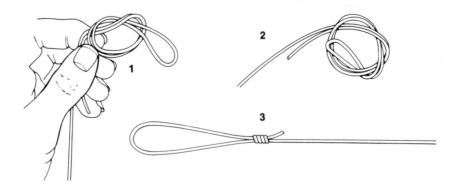

Use this knot to tie a loop in the end of a line for attaching leaders, sinkers or other terminal gear quickly.

1. Double back a few inches of line and tie it into an overhand knot.
2. Leave the overhand knot open and bring the doubled line through once again.
3. Hold the standing line and tag end and pull on the loop to tighten the knot. The size of the loop formed can be controlled by positioning the loose knot and holding it while the knot is tightened. Clip tag end.

Simplified blood knot

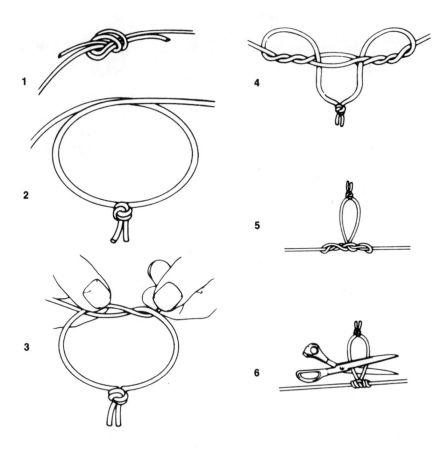

Used to tie two pieces of line or leader together, this knot works best when the lines are equal or nearly equal in diameter.

1. Take the two line ends and tie a simple overhand knot and pull it tight. This will be clipped off later.
2. Form a loop where the two lines meet, with the overhand knot hanging free, as shown.
3. Pull one side of the loop down and begin taking turns with it around the standing line. This is easier to do than described. Keep the place where the lines join open so the number of turns on each side is equal.
4. After making eight or ten turns, reach through the center opening and pull the overhand knot through. Put your finger in this loop so it doesn't slip out.
5. Hold the overhand knot with your teeth, take your finger away and pull on both ends of the line, creating tight coils.
6. Let go with your teeth and pull hard to set the knot firmly. The overhand knot loop will stick out 90 degrees. Clip off the excess close to the joining knot.

Snelling a hook

1   **2**   **3**

Years ago factory-snelled hooks were common. Today, fishermen prefer to buy loose hooks and leader material of their own choice and tie the snells themselves to suit bait fishing needs.
1. Pass one end of the leader through the eye and past the hook bend. Pass the other end of the leader through the eye in the opposite direction, leaving a large loop.
2. Hold both lines along the shank. Use the line hanging from the eye and wind tight coils around the shank and both lines, starting at the eye and working toward the bend. Make 5 or 10 neat turns.
3. Hold the coils and pull on the long leader end until the entire loop disappears under the coils, and pull the coils snug.
4. Hold the tag end with pliers and the leader in your other hand, and pull in opposite directions to tighten the snell securely. Clip off the tag end and tie a surgeon's end loop in the end of the leader.

Surgeon's knot

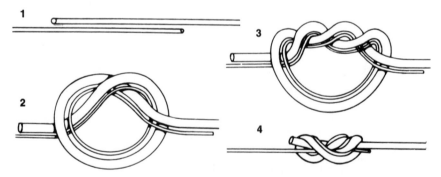

1   **2**   **3**   **4**

This knot can be used to join two lines of different diameters.
1. Lay the line and leader parallel with an overlap of about eight inches.
2. Treat the two lines as a single line and tie an overhand knot, passing the entire leader through the loop. Leave the loop open.
3. Make a second overhand knot, again passing the whole leader and overlapped line through.
4. Hold both overlaps and pull in opposite directions to make the knot. Then pull the line only against the leader to set the knot. Clip the surplus ends close to the knot.

Uni-knot

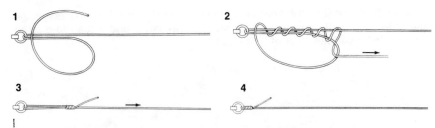

A knot with many variations and applications. The basic uni-knot is shown here: It is excellent for tying on hooks, swivels and lures.
1. Run the line through the eye at least six inches and fold it back against the standing line. Bring the tag end back in a circle to form a loop as shown.
2. Make six turns with the tag end around the two lines and through the circle. Hold the two lines at the eye and pull on the tag end to snug up the turns.
3. Now pull on the standing line to slide the knot against the eye.
4. Continue pulling until the knot is good and tight. Trim the tag end flush with the last coil.

Trilene knot

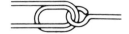

1. Run end of line through eye of hook or lure and double back through the eye a second time.

2. Loop around standing part of line 5 or 6 times.

3. Thread tag end back between the eye and the coils as shown.

4. Pull up tight and trim tag end.

The Trilene Knot is an all-purpose connection to join mono to swivels, snaps, hooks and artificial lures. The knot's unique design and ease of tying yield consistently strong, dependable connections while retaining 85-90% of the original line strength. The double wrap of mono through the eyelet provides a protective cushion for added safety.

Palomar Knot

The Palomar Knot is a favorite of light tackle anglers because it is easy to tie, yet is exceptionally strong and resistant to breaking under the rapid strain caused from sudden runs of hefty fish.

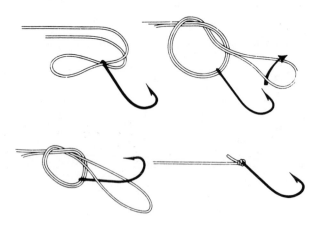

Dropper Loop

The Dropper Loop is an old time knot that is still popular today. It is used to tie a loop(s) in the leader for adding hooks, short leaders and even sinkers. Many fishermen prefer using a three way swivel, but for a simple rig with minimal hardware, the dropper loop is indispensable.

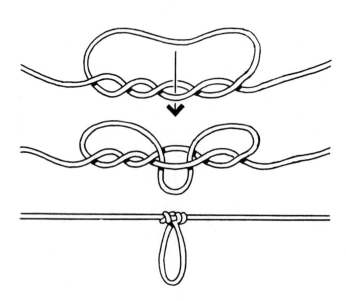

Standard One-Hook Rig

The standard one-hook rig may be used for both bay and ocean fluke fishing and is also the preferred rig for trolling. A wide variety of bait may be used, but a single strip of squid, or squid and baitfish combination, is the most effective. Strip baits or large baits may be fished effectively with the substitution of a tandem hook for a single hook.

Take a 48-inch length of 30-pound test nylon leader material. Attach a 1/0 black swivel to one end with an improved clinch knot, and tie an end loop two inches long to the opposite end. Make a dropper loop in the leader six to twelve inches above the bottom of the end loop. The distance should be six inches when fishing in shallow water or over a clear sandy bottom, twelve inches for ocean fishing or when the bottom is rough in order to reduce the number of hang-ups. After all knots have been tied, the completed leader should be between 36 and 42 inches in length.

Use a 2/0 gold beak hook when fishing in shallow water or where small fish predominate, a 4/0 gold beak hook when fishing in deep water or over wrecks where medium and large fluke are apt to be found. Snell the hook with 30-lb. test leader material. Tie a one-inch end loop at the end of the snell 36 to 42 inches from the hook.

To attach the snelled hook to the leader, simply pass the one-inch end loop over the dropper loop. Then pass the point of the hook through the dropper loop (from underneath) and pull the snell through until the dropper loop and the end loop mesh together. The standard one-hook rig is now complete. Attach it to the main line with an improved clinch-knot.

If the rig is fished too far behind the boat so that the line enters the water at a very shallow angle, the length of line between the dropper loop and the sinker loses its effectiveness in keeping the bait off the bottom. As such, this rig should be fished as vertical as possible, which can be achieved by adding additional sinker weight.

High-Low Rig

A high-low rig is nothing more than adding a second hook to the previously described standard one-hook rig. However, depending on the second species being sought, and if you're using a tight trolling pattern, some modification to the original one-hook rig is necessary. Let's assume that you're trolling or drifting for fluke where double-headers are a frequent occurrence (it makes for some interesting fishing when you have two five-pound fluke on at the same time, and each wants to go in a different direction). For this type of high-low fluke rig, use the same end loop for your sinker, and place the first dropper loop 6 inches up the line. However, instead of using a 36-inch long snell on the first dropper, shorten the leader length to 18 inches. Twelve inches above the first dropper, tie a second dropper to which is added a snelled hook on a six-inch leader.

With the suggested shortened leaders, you tend to avoid tangles when making tight turns, the two baits are fairly close together as they come through the water, thus resembling a small school of baitfish, and since fluke tend to pocket closely together, double-headers are not unusual.

If weakfish or seabass are in the area, increase the distance between the first and second dropper to 2-3 feet as these species tend to swim above the bottom, and are easy victims for a pennant-shaped strip of squid or a whole sandworm hooked once through its head which allows the tail to swim naturally.

One-hook rig

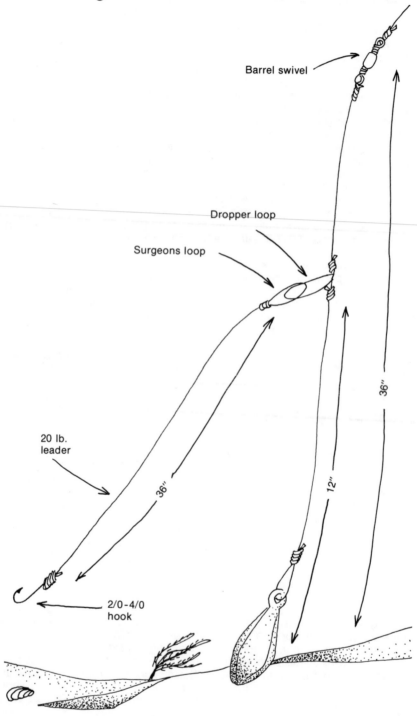

Barrel swivel

Dropper loop

Surgeons loop

20 lb. leader

36"

36"

12"

2/0-4/0 hook

High-low rig

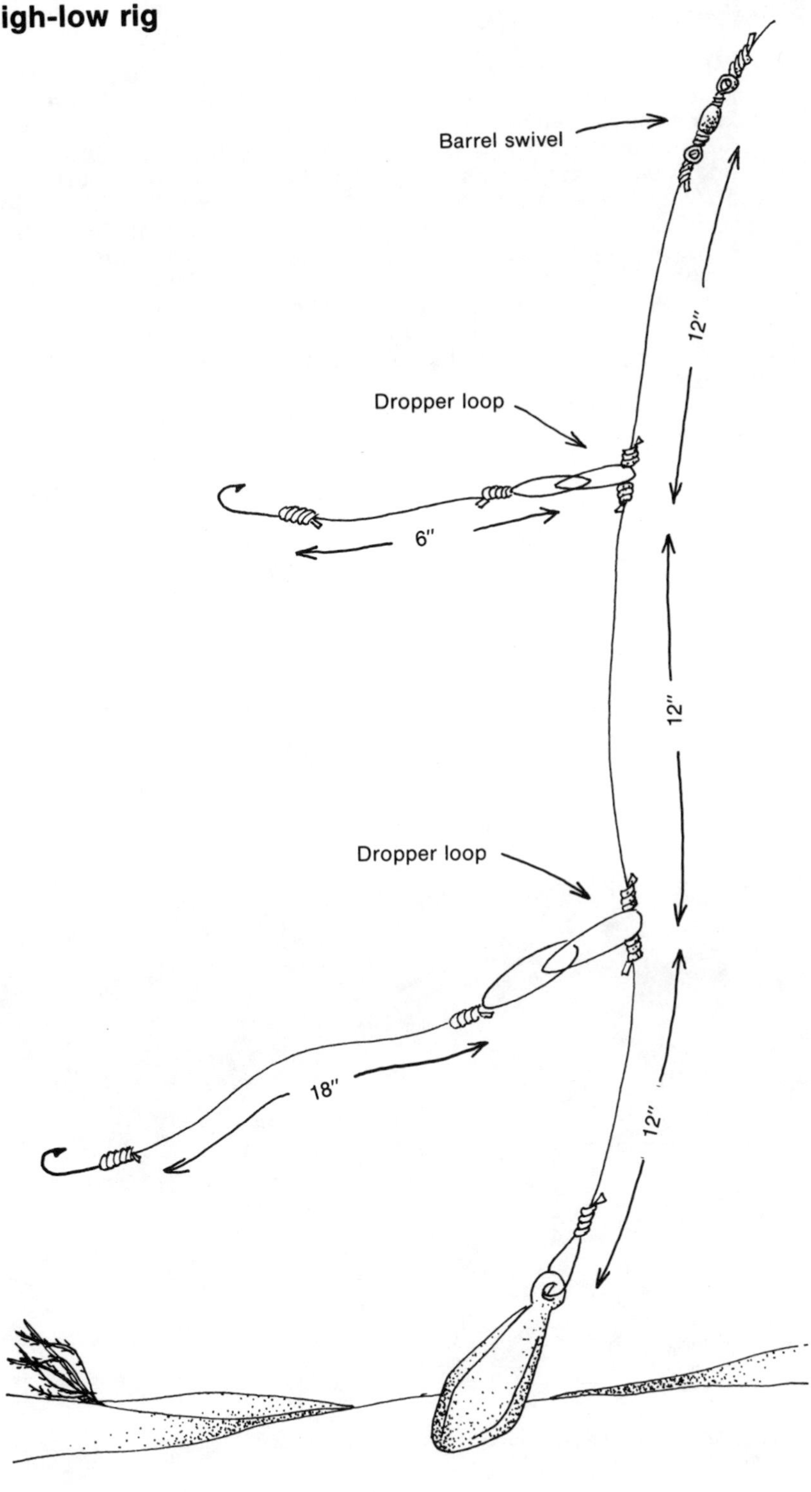

Barrel swivel

12"

Dropper loop

6"

12"

Dropper loop

12"

18"

Fish-Finder Rig

One of the disadvantages of using the previously mentioned standard one-hook or high-low rigs, is that the fluke may feel the unnatural weight of the sinker before you can feel the drag of the fish. This is especially true when the fluke are not feeding aggressively, and are just playing with the bait. Borrowing a page from the surf fisherman's handbook, it's suggested that you use a fish-finder rig when you want to feel the fluke *BEFORE* he feels you.

The advantages of the fish-finder rig are two-fold. First, with the line passing directly through the fish-finder rig, neither you nor the fish are hampered by the weight of the sinker. Secondly, you can change sinker weights easily as you encounter different water depths. The ease of sinker changing is a definite improvement over using an egg-type sinker where the line runs through the weight, and has to be cut whenever the weight is switched to another size.

The components for making this rig are a #5 or #7 barrel swivel, 2/0 or 3/0 wide-gap hook, 36-inch length of 30-pound test leader material and a fish-finder rig. Snell the hook with the leader material and attach the barrel swivel to the opposite end with either an improved clinch or Palomar knot. The fish-finder rig is then threaded onto the main line which, in turn, is attached to the barrel swivel with an improved clinch. The sinker is then added to the fish-finder rig and you're all set for drag-free fluke fishing. If the area you are fishing requires the bait to be suspended above the bottom, you can add a small, round-clip-on float to the leader. The nearer you mount the float to the hook, the higher the bait will ride above the bottom.

Bucktails are traditional but plastic skirts and flourescent tubing are new additions to the fluker's arsenal.

Fish-finder rig

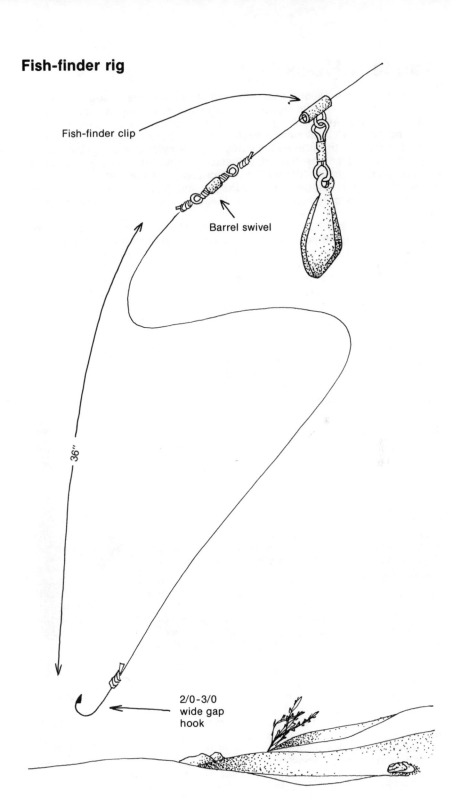

Fish-finder clip

Barrel swivel

36"

2/0-3/0
wide gap
hook

Tandem Hook Rigs

This rig was designed to overcome the problem of the fluke's tendency to bite a large baitfish or strip bait "short," either mangling or stealing the angler's bait entirely without touching the hook. The tandem hook fluke rig places a second "stinger" hook near the tail of the baitfish or the end of a strip bait in such a manner that the bait will not become twisted in a moving current. It also has the advantage of being adjustable so that the same rig may be used for strip baits of varying lengths. The effectiveness of a tandem hook for fluke is remarkable, and can be shown by the percentage of the catch taken on the stinger hook. In a typical catch of 10 fluke, eight will be taken on the stinger hook.

The only materials necessary to tie a tandem hook rig are a 42-inch length of 30-pound leader material and a 3/0 and 5/0 gold beak hook. The 3/0 hook is attached to the snell permanently and the 5/0 stinger hook is threaded onto the snell below it with a small knot preventing it from slipping off. This "stinger" hook floats freely on the line so that it may be adjusted to the length of the bait, and also may revolve to prevent the strip bait or baitfish from becoming twisted and moving unnaturally. It may seem difficult to tie at first, but with a little practice is really quite simple. Just follow the steps with the accompanying diagram and you will get the knack of it in no time.

STEP ONE. Tie a figure-8 knot at one end of the leader material. This is done by forming a loop with a one-inch diameter and passing the end of the line through its center twice. Then the loop is slowly pulled taut, forming a knot that will prevent the stinger hook from sliding off the end of the snell. Tie the figure-8 knot close enough to the end so that at least 36 inches of snell remains above it.

STEP TWO. Clip the excess leader material below the knot. Leave at least a sixteenth of an inch to allow for any slippage.

STEP THREE. Thread the 5/0 gold beak hook on the snell and slide it down to the knot. This is the sliding "stinger" knot.

STEP FOUR. Tie a second figure-8 knot approximately four to five inches above the first but do not pull it taut. Instead, grasp the loop with the thumb and index fingers of both hands and twist them a quarter-turn in opposite directions so that you now have two smaller loops in the shape of an eight. Grasp the figure-8 in its center with the thumb and index finger of the left hand to hold the shape while executing step five.

STEP FIVE. Insert the point of the 3/0 gold beak hook through both loops of the figure-8 knot. The point should enter the same side of each loop as the line that extends from each end of the figure-8 knot. Then thread the end of the line through the eye of the hook and slowly pull the figure-8 knot taut around the shank. When properly tied, the shank of the hook will be parallel with the line running towards the stinger hook as shown in the last diagram, which is the finished product.

The tandem hook can be attached to the same leader that is used for the standard one-hook rig, the bottom loop of the high-low rig or the fish-finder rig. The single hook should always be replaced with a tandem hook whenever fishing strip baits or large baitfish.

An alternative to tying your own tandem hook rigs, is to purchase a quantity of Mustad Ryder hooks model #92586. This is a long shank hook which has a smaller hook soldered near the eye of the hook. The head of any bait is placed on the smaller hook, while the tail is placed on the larger (or stinger) hook. While the two hooks aren't adjustable in terms of distance between the two, you can avoid some tying hassle by using this type of hook.

Tandem hook rig

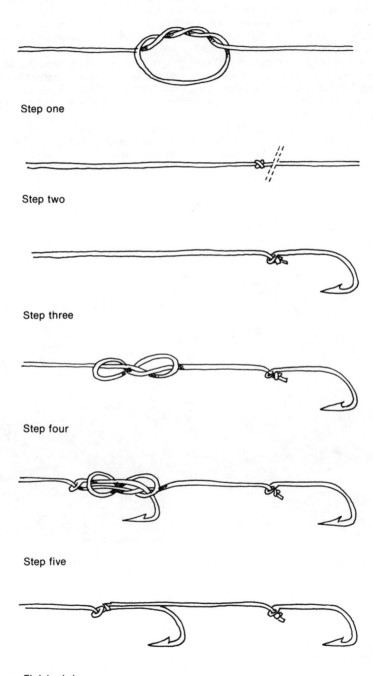

Step one

Step two

Step three

Step four

Step five

Finished rig

Float or Bobber Rig

The float or bobber rig is one of the least used among fluke fishermen, but under certain fishing conditions it is often extremely effective. It consists of a single snelled hook baited with a live baitfish with a float or bobber attached several feet above. The float may be moved and the distance between it and the hook adjusted without re-rigging.

This rig is very effective when fishing over shallow flats where the fluke are wary and may be spooked by the hull of a boat looming over their heads. The float will carry the rig away from the boat while, at the same time, preventing the baitfish from hiding in obstructions on the bottom so that it will be visible and vulnerable to foraging fluke.

The float rig also gives the pier or jetty fisherman a degree of mobility that he doesn't have with other rigs. The float can be used to "walk" the baitfish out with the current, allowing the angler to cover more bottom in search of a fluke while at the same time giving the bait some movement.

The float rig should only be used in water shallow enough to keep the bait within two or three feet from the bottom within the fluke's feeding range. It's a good idea to add one or two small split shot about a foot above the hook to discourage the baitfish from swimming near the surface. Tie the snell of the hook to the other end of your line with an improved clinch knot. Attach the float above the hook approximately the same distance as the depth of the water.

Jack and Judy Graham make a great husband and wife fluke fishing team.

Ready-Made Rigs

In this chapter, we've been discussing how to construct your own fluke rigs. If, however, you don't have the patience or the time to design and build your own rigs, you can purchase ready-made rigs at most tackle stores, boat liveries and marinas. It's even a good idea to pick up a few ready-made rigs to give you some idea as to how the professional tiers do it. There are many excellent "factory-made" rigs available that do very well on fluke.

Float rig

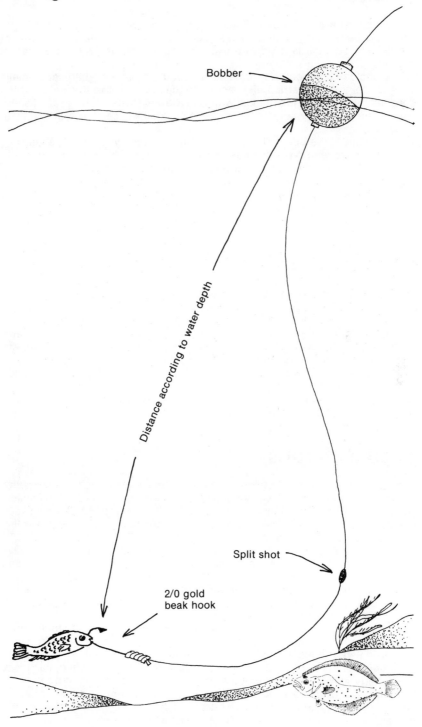

Bobber

Distance according to water depth

Split shot

2/0 gold beak hook

Bucktail Rig

A variation of the standard fluke rig that works very well to attract larger fish is the bucktail rig. Instead of a sinker to get the rig to the dining room of the fluke. a bucktail is used to provide weight to take the rig to the bottom depths.

The bucktail adds color, a realistic silhouette, a baitfish shape and smells like the real thing if a strip bait is added to the hook. Unlike the sinker which does not have a hook, the bucktail will take a few extra fish during each fishing day. In fact there are many times when the bucktail will catch the largest fluke of the day.

The weight of the bucktail should be similar to what you would usually use for a sinker. Depending on the tide or current flow and the water depth, bucktails from ¾ ounce to 3 ounces will be the most common to use.

Many shapes of bucktails are available, but the round headed bucktail known as the "Musketball" has the most mass and will get down the fastest and with the least water resistance. Other anglers, however, use the lima bean, Smilin' Bill or bullet shaped heads with success.

Feather Rigs

While many fluke experts disdain the use of any extra material on their rigs, preferring to keep the rig as simple as possible, there are other flukers who swear that some additives to the rigs will add to their fish catching ability.

Simple additives like saddle hackles (chicken feathers), bucktail hair and the new nylon imitation hair called Fish Hair can improve some rigs. Feathers and hair materials are available in most tackle shops in the fly tying department and are very inexpensive. Both are tied directly to the hook to add shape, color and a larger profile for the bait.

Tiny plastic skirts are now available that not only add color and motion but even have flourescence built into them, and are definitely worth a try.

Miscellaneous

Inventive flukers have been seeking ways to make their rigs more attractive for over a century. While many years ago there was a trend to add shiny beads, spinner blades and other "hardware" to fluke rigs, the trend today is to keep the rigs as simple as possible. Too much hardware can actually spook the fish and diminish the day's catch.

There are times, however, when a small spinner blade may have a positive effect on fishing. Areas where waters are muddied or discolored by strong tides or recent rains may experience better catches with the addition of something shiny to help attract the attention of a fluke. One or two chromed or pearlescent beads placed on the leader just ahead of the hook will also work under these off-color water conditions.

Summer flounder anglers who tie saddle hackles or bucktail to their hooks add a thin strip of mylar, a plastic material with a metallic and very shiny silver or gold finish. It adds a touch of flash that makes a rather plain rig look like a live smelt or spearing as it swims in the current. Often this hint of flash may fool a hefty fish, or even school sized fish, into striking a baited hook.

Adding hardware to a rig takes some careful thought. Adding spinners, beads or mylar for no reason may hurt the fish catching ability of a rig, but that same additive may prove to be successful when used at a minimum.

Bucktail rig

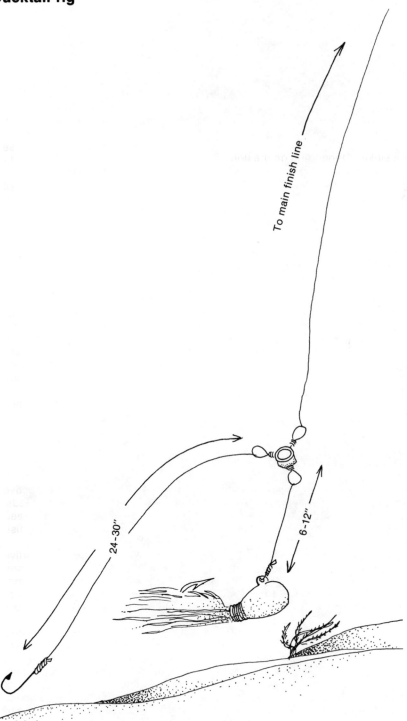

To main finish line

24–30"

6–12"

5
THE MENU

"Menu" is the appropriate word whenever the subject of baits for fluke is discussed. Just as the fisherman has his favorite entrees on a restaurant menu and likes an occasional change of pace, so does the fluke. What fluke may "order" at a given time will be determined by several factors that the angler must contend with. What are they feeding on? What are the prevailing wind and current conditions? How will they combine to affect the presentation of various baits?

When the angler leaves the dock for a day of fluke fishing, he usually doesn't know what bait the fish will be taking on that particular day. Therefore, you should always make it a practice to bring two or more baits so that you may offer the fluke a choice. I carry squid and at least one baitfish (killies, sand eels or spearing) to start the day's fishing. After a short time, usually a small fluke, sea robin or bergall will be caught that may be cut into strip baits and added to the menu. Rig up each line in the water with a different bait until the fluke show a preference for one over the other, then switch all rigs to the "hot" bait.

Fluke will usually be feeding on whatever food source is most abundant and easy to catch. If schools of sand eels can be seen in the water, it's a safe bet that the fluke are gorging themselves on sand eels. Keep a watchful eye on what the fluke are spitting out on the deck as they try to throw the hook. Cut a fluke open and examine the stomach contents. Is it crammed with sand eels? Spearing? Killies? An empty stomach is usually a good sign — food is scarce, so the fluke should be hungry and take a variety of baits with little preference.

An abundance of a particular baitfish in the water can also have a negative effect — the fluke will gorge themselves for a couple of days and become bored with the menu. Then they will often pounce on another food that passes by, even if they aren't hungry, just to break up the monotony. So, the trick is to experiment and improvise with bait until you find the right combination. Don't fall into the trap of using a particular bait exclusively because you did a number on the fluke with it once before.

After the preferred bait has been determined, the manner in which it is rigged is critical. To understand why, you must first understand the two different methods in which fluke feed: by forage and ambush.

When fluke are "foraging," they are on the move in search of food. They will often move up and down the length of a rip or along a channel, watching for signs of movement. When a baitfish is spotted, the fluke pursues with a quick burst of speed, usually catching the fleeing fish tail first. Unless the baitfish is very small, in which case it will be swallowed quickly, the fluke will just grab it by the tail and hold on until the baitfish stops struggling, then slowly start chewing his way up the body in small increments. Knowing this, the angler must always be certain when using large strip baits that there is a hook in the tail portion. This is when a tandem or Ryder hook combination is especially effective.

Fluke will also lie in ambush for a meal, particularly the doormats that have to compete with the faster, smaller fish for the available food supply. They will lie motionless and change their pigmentation to blend in with the composition of the bottom. Fluke normally face up-current because baitfish will always travel down-current, the course of least resistance.

Contrary to popular belief, fluke do not always rest completely flat on the bottom. They support themselves slightly off the bottom on their dorsal and anal fins, which allows them a quick getaway after prey. When an unwary baitfish comes within striking distance, the fluke gives a powerful thrust of the tail and is upon the baitfish before it has a chance to respond.

When will fluke employ the ambush technique of feeding? Well, it can be just about any time, but it more likely will be when the water clarity is extremely good or the prey is excessively fast. If the fluke is feeding on sand eels in a calm surf over a sandy bottom on a bright day, he'll be forced to rely on ambush to keep his belly full. The fluke must also ambush the speedy snappers (baby bluefish), which they can't possibly hope to catch by pursuit. In any case, the important point here for the angler is that an ambushing fluke will always attack the prey at the largest target presented — the mid-body. If the angler rigs a snapper with hooks in head and tail, the reward will often be a head on one hook and the tail on the other without a body between to join them together. So, when fishing with whole snappers, the stinger hook of the tandem rig must be placed at mid-body, rather than in the tail portion, in order to adjust to the fluke's feeding habits.

Regardless of the bait that is being used, it must be rigged so it will be presented in a natural manner. What is a natural manner? Well, the bait should look and move as if it is alive. The bait should not spin in the current, nor should it be twisted or bunched up on the hook.

Let's take a hook at some of the more effective fluke baits and when they should be used, availability and how they can be rigged for the most natural presentation.

Killies

The killie is a hardy baitfish 1½ to 4 inches in length that is easily kept alive with a minimum amount of effort. They are readily available at bait and tackle shops, or the angler may catch his own with a bait trap of seine. Their natural habitat is the shallow water of bays and estuaries. They are rarely found in the ocean except during seasonal migrations. For this reason, killies are most effective in bays and inlets where they are a primary part of the fluke's diet, but poor producers in the ocean. As a rule, they will not take a high percentage of large fish. But the fact that killies are the only baitfish that may be easily obtained and kept alive make them one of the most popular and effective baits for fluke.

Killies can be kept alive for long periods of time in a live bait car or for shorter periods when kept moist with a layer of seaweed and kept out of the rays of the sun.

When drifting or trolling, the killie should be hooked lightly through both lips so that it is capable of swimming freely, and will stay alive and active as long as possible. Even when dead, the killie makes an excellent bait when combined with a bucktail and bounced along the bottom. When using the bucktail/killie combination, the bait should be again hooked through both lips. The bucktail will provide the flash to attract the fluke, and the killie will produce the scent to make the fluke want to feed.

Another combination that is very popular is to combine a killie and a strip of squid on the same hook. The sandwich bait, as it is called, is very effective but the baits must be hooked in the proper sequence to achieve the best results. The strip of squid should be placed on the hook first, followed by the killie. The Rationale for this sequence is that the wiggling killie acts as an attractor for the fluke and the long fluttering piece of squid gives the fluke something to strike and hold on to. If the hooking sequence were reversed, the squid strip would cover the live killie.

When the fluke trip is over, you can take your unused killies home and freeze them in double plastic freezer bags. When thawed at room temperature, these frozen killies become an excellent bait in both fresh and salt water if hooked through the lips and twitched along the bottom using a light spinning rod.

Killies are a long time favorite bait, especially for bay fishermen. They can be hooked a variety of ways as shown in the above photo.

Sand Eels

Also known as "sand launce," sand eels are the most productive of bait-fish for fluke, which eat them like candy. This is undoubtedly due to the fact that sand eels comprise a large percentage of the fluke's diet in both the ocean and inshore waters, particularly early in the season when large schools of sand eels visit our inshore waters. Sand eels are readily available in frozen form at bait and tackle outlets, but they are much more effective when fresh. The freezing process breaks down the flesh, rendering it somewhat mushy, and it is not uncommon for the belly to burst when defrosted. The angler can easily obtain his own supply of fresh, firm sand eels with an umbrella net or seine.

There are several methods of rigging sand eels for fluke. If the sand eels on hand are three to four inches in length, they may either be hooked through the eye sockets or under the mouth and out the snout. Large sand eels of five to eight inches should be rigged on a tandem hook; top hook through the eye sockets and stinger hook in the tail section. Small baitfish can also be used effectively by placing two on the top hook and two on the stinger hook through the eye sockets to simulate a small school of baitfish.

Another little-known trick is to pinch off the head of a sand eel to release more of the bait's scent, and then hooking the remaining body on the tail end of a bucktail. Again, the bucktail provides the weight to get the bait to the bottom as well as providing the flash, and the sand eel provides the target strike area for the fluke.

Fresh spearing are hard to beat for summer flounder and can be fished along with a strip of squid if desired.

Spearing

Also known as "silversides," spearing are usually purchased frozen. They are virtually impossible to keep alive, but the angler should still make the attempt to obtain a fresh supply for fluke fishing with the aid of a seine or umbrella net. Fresh spearing are firm and stay on the hook well, but the frozen variety become mushy and difficult to keep on the hook when thawed. They range in size from 1½ to 5 inches, and usually a frozen package will consist of baitfish that are all the same size. Care should be taken to purchase the largest spearing available.

There are several ways of placing the spearing on a hook. The smaller baitfish of 2 to 3 inches may either be hooked through the eyes or under the mouth and out the snout. Large spearing 3 to 5 inches should be fished with a tandem hook rig with the 3/0 top hook through the eyes and the 5/0 stinger hook embedded near the tail. Small baitfish may also be fished on the tandem hook to give the appearance of a small school of baitfish. Place two or three small spearing on each hook through the eyes.

Large spearing are an excellent bait for fluke in both bay and ocean fishing, where they are a primary part of the fluke's diet because of their abundance. Large fresh-caught spearing are also an extremely effective bait when properly trolled.

Incidentally, if spearing are in good supply in your area, you should purchase bucktails that have strips of silver mylar down their sides, as this is the exact profile of a fleeing spearing, and should produce more fluke hits.

Smelt

Smelt are anadromous fish that spawn in fresh water but live in salt water. They are excellent bait for ocean fluke fishing where medium and large fish can be expected. The smelt's round body and five to eight-inch length make it the largest baitfish readily available to the angler. The frozen seafood department in most large supermarkets carry them, in two forms — whole-round and dressed. You want the whole-round for fluke fishing, as the dressed smelt have had their heads and entrails removed.

Use of a tandem hook is mandatory when smelt are used for bait. They have very small mouths, so don't worry about them opening and causing an unnatural movement from water resistance — they won't. Pass the top hook through the eye sockets and embed the stinger hook through the body no more than two inches from the tail.

When using large baits such as smelt, you have to allow the fluke a little more time to mouth the bait before you set the hook. Some anglers count to 10, others to 20, and others wait until they feel a steady pull on the line before setting the hook . . . the choice is yours as there is no hard and fast rule about hook-setting.

Snappers

Snappers, which are baby bluefish, infest our waters from July to October and are undoubtedly the most deadly fluke bait that the angler may obtain by himself. The fisherman can fish for snappers for a few minutes before the boat leaves the dock and catch the day's supply of live bait. During August and September, snappers are a primary food source for fluke as they feed and prepare for the offshore migration. Large doormat fluke have a particular fondness for live snappers.

Snappers are kept alive and active in a live bait well with circulating sea water. Aerators will also do the job efficiently, but care should be taken on hot days to make sure that the water doesn't increase in temperature too rapidly and stun the fragile snappers with thermal shock. A large plastic garbage can can also be used, but the water should be changed frequently to maintain a high oxygen content and relatively steady temperature. Small quantities of snappers can be carried in a live bait car when the boat is not in motion.

If the circumstances do not permit you to use live snappers, fresh-dead or even frozen ones will also get the job done. The trick is to get the snapper to die with its gills closed. When snappers die as a result of being taken out of the water and left in the air or slowly drowned in a small bucket of water, there is a natural tendency for the gills to flare open. This flaring would cause the fish to have an unnatural appearance and movement, making it a poor bait for fluke. Snappers should therefore be killed immediately after being taken out of the water by applying direct pressure to the head. If this doesn't work and the gills remain open, cut the head off immediately behind the gills and just fish the body.

There are many ways of rigging both live and dead snappers for fluke. All are effective as long as one hook is embedded somewhere near the middle of the body, the portion at which an attacking fluke is most likely to strike. In slow-moving currents, shallow waters or from the surf, snappers may be live-lined by placing a single 3/0 gold beak hook between the first and second dorsal fin. Embed the point just deep enough to keep the snapper on the hook, taking care not to injure the fish or impede its movement.

A tandem hook rig should be used when fishing live snappers in a fast current or when there is a moderately fast drift due to wind conditions. The single hook behind the dorsal fin will exert a sideways pulling force on the snapper at these times, impeding his natural movement considerably. The top hook should be hooked slightly through the upper lip and the stinger hook placed between the dorsal fins as described.

Whole dead snappers should also be fished with a tandem hook rig. The top hook should be embedded firmly through both lips, bottom lip first. This will prevent the snapper's mouth from opening, creating water resistance that will result in unnatural body movements. Once again, the stinger hook is placed between the dorsal fins. If the snapper has been frozen and the body has become stiff, slowly bend it several times so that it will have a little more elasticity and the moving water can give it a little natural movement. Whenever possible, use fresh-dead snappers, but keep them wet so that the skin does not become dry and wrinkled.

If you are using snappers that have had the heads removed, a single 3/0 gold beak hook may be used if the fish are small. Hook the snapper through the center of the body near the cut. Make sure that the body does not spin when placed in the water. When using a tandem hook rig on the larger snapper bodies, the stinger hook can be placed at mid-body between the dorsal fins. *DO NOT* place the hook near the lateral line . . . the hook will not be able to penetrate quickly if the body of the snapper fills the bend of the hook.

Snapper blues, and snapper blue belly strips, are great fluke baits, but are often overlooked by most anglers.

Squid

The most versatile bait for fluke is squid, which may be used in a variety of ways effectively. It is easily purchased in any bait and tackle outlet or local fish market, and the freezing process doesn't change its characteristics. As a rule, the angler is better off purchasing his supply of squid in a fish market even though the price is often higher. The reasons for this are threefold: the squid is fresh and, unlike much of the frozen variety which comes from California, was taken from local waters. The angler also has the option of selecting the size of the squid he is purchasing to use as bait for fluke.

The most popular method of using squid is in strip form with a baitfish, often called a combination bait, ham and eggs, or sandwich bait. The squid is first cleaned by severing the head and slitting the mantle open so that it lies flat. It is then cut into pennant shapes three to four inches long and a half to three-quarters of an inch wide, tapering to a point. The squid strip is placed on the hook by embedding the point of the hook through the wide end and no more than a half-inch from the top. This allows the strip to flutter enticingly in the current. *DO NOT* hook the squid strip more than once, to prevent spinning. It may be used in combination with a killie, spearing or sand eel. For combination baits it is best to purchase squid with a mantle length of four inches. Larger squid six inches or longer may be used by cutting the mantle into equal halves before cutting into strips.

Large squid cut into long strips is also an extremely effective bait for fluke. Use long squid strips with a tandem or Ryder hook. The top hook is placed no more than one-half inch down from the wide end, and the stinger hook is embedded no more than one-and-a-half inches above the tapered end of the strip.

The most effective way of using squid for big fluke is whole, but this is often impractical when there is an abundance of small fish around. Small fluke have no qualms about attacking a squid approaching their own size, so too many squid would be mangled and wasted to make their use worthwhile. The time to use whole squid is in late summer and fall when the doormat class of fluke is more in evidence as they fatten up for their migration. Whole squid *MUST* be rigged up with a tandem hook or Ryder rig for best results. The top hook is embedded in the mantle between the wings through the plastic-like backbone about a half-inch from the top. The stinger hook is embedded through the eyes or further up the mantle, depending on the size of the squid.

Small, tapered strips of squid are also excellent for artificials that are being worked for fluke. Strips three to four inches long not only add more natural flutter to an artificial, but also give off an enticing aroma. White bucktails, Hopkins and lead-headed plastic shrimp are all more effective when tipped with a strip of squid.

Rather than cutting up squid when you should be fishing for fluke on a boat or beach, I'd suggest that you cut up a supply of squid strips a few days before a trip and place them in a Tupper-ware type container in the freezer. Be sure to label the containers. You need only enough squid strips in each container to start you off for the day. After you've caught a few fluke, sharks or other miscellaneous fish, you can cut strips from these species and use these alternatives as your bait. A good way of keeping squid strips fresh and cool while fishing on a hot jetty or boat is to place the bait, while still partially frozen, in a wide-mouth thermos-type container. The double-insulated walls of such a container will keep the cut squid cool, and prevent it from turning into a pile of mush that won't stay on your hook. If your squid strips begin to turn soft and off-color, add some salt water to the container. Don't use the water adjacent to the boat launching area as this water tends to contain fuel and oil. Clear salt water will help toughen up the strips as well as turning them white in color.

Squid, cut into strips, is the universal bait for summer flounder no matter where you live along the Atlantic coast.

The "ham and cheese" of the fluke world; a live killie and a strip of squid is a deadly combination.

Small, whole squid are fished for large fluke called doormats because of their huge size. Use a Ryder style hook to hold the bait properly.

Strip Baits

There must be something absolutely tantalizing about a strip bait slowly gliding over the bottom because a fluke can't seem to resist it. Strip baits have numerous advantages over baitfish: they will remain intact on the hook through multiple strikes, yield large baits, are in constant supply and are minutes fresh . . . all at little or no expense to the angler. Another advantage of fishing strip baits is the fact that they will take doormat fluke of 14 pounds as easily as they will take fish of 14 inches. As a rule, strip baits are usually more effective in deep water areas such as found around the mouths of inlets, ocean wrecks and shoals and tidal rips where fluke are accustomed to feeding on larger baitfish than normally found in the shallower water of the bays.

When fishing with small baitfish, the angler usually has only one crack at a striking fish. If the angler strikes too early and the fluke doesn't have the hook in his mouth, the baitfish will usually either be bitten off behind the head or pulled off the hook entirely. But it's a rare day of fishing when the fluke will be capable of "stealing" a strip bait with any semblance of regularity without meeting the business end of a hook. The angler will often have two, three or more shots at a striking fish, thereby increasing the chances of hooking up.

All strip baits require the use of a tandem or Ryder hook rig. Fluke will take a strip bait tail first more than 80% of the time, making it mandatory to have a "stinger" hook in the end of the strip. Strip baits should be cut as large as practical and rigged in the following manner regardless of length: the top hook should be hooked through the center of the wide end of the strip no more than a half-inch from the end. If it is, the top of the strip will fold down and it may begin to spin or twist in the current. The "stinger" hook should be embedded in the tail of the strip *NO MORE* than two inches from the end.

It it extremely critical that the strip bait does not have a bend in the middle that could result in an unnatural spinning movement in the current. This belly will occur if the stinger hook is placed further away from the top hook than the length of the leader between the tandem hooks allows. To measure the point at which the stinger hook should be embedded in the strip bait, place the top hook in the strip first previously described. Then lay the line and stinger hook on top of the strip and straighten them out so everything is parallel. The lowest point on the strip that the bend of the stinger hook falls on is where the stinger hook should be embedded. When held up by the leader, the strip bait should hang perfectly straight without any bend. If the strip bait isn't long enough to fill the gap between the tandem hooks, slide the stinger hook up the line and embed it one or two inches from the tip. Don't worry about the visibility of the protruding hooks — fluke are very rarely hook-shy.

Fluke "Belly"

The fluke itself provides the best all-around strip bait. Long, flat, pennant-shaped strip baits cut from a small fluke (often referred to as "fluke belly") glide naturally through the current with an enticing flutter. The fluke that are caught provide the angler with a fresh supply of bait right at his fingertips. Small fluke 12 to 14 inches in length are the ideal size for cutting strip baits. Keep in mind the legal lengths of fluke in various states.

Very little practice is necessary to cut up perfect strip baits from a fluke. All that is necessary is a sharp fillet knife and a little patience. Lay the fluke light side up on a flat surface. Then lift the pectoral fin and make a vertical cut behind it down to the bones.

Make a cut from the vertical cut to the tail along the lateral line, which marks the backbone. Starting at the vertical cut, make three more cuts three-quarters of an inch wide tapering to a point at the tail. This will create three pennant-shaped strip baits that are still attached to the bones.

To sever the strip baits from the bones, insert the blade of the fillet knife into the cut along the lateral line near the vertical cut. Then turn the blade so that it is flat with the bones and begin making long, sweeping cuts towards the tail until the strip bait detaches. Repeat the process until all the flesh from both the dark and white sides of the fluke has been cut into strips.

One fluke will yield eight to twelve baits, depending on its size. Both dark and white strips are effective, and the individual angler perferring one over the other. The strips from the outermost edge of the fluke are the most effective because they're thin and flutter enticingly.

Fluke belly is rigged on a tandem or Ryder hook rig, with the top hook embedded in the wide end no more than a half-inch down from the top, and the stinger hook placed between 1½ and 2 inches above the point of the taper. Pre-cut strip baits may be frozen for future trips, but the flesh tends to become mushy. The best bet is to freeze the fluke whole and cut the strip baits during the fishing trip as they are needed. As long as the flesh is attached to the bones, it will remain firm and pliable. Care should be taken to keep fluke that are being used for bait out of the sun to prevent the skin from becoming dried out and wrinkled. It's a good idea to keep fish and strip baits covered with a wet rag or towel.

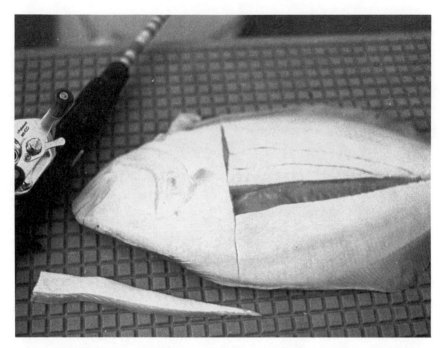

Fluke belly strips, and back strips too, frequently outcatch every other type of bait and many flukers will sacrifice their fish to get a supply of bait.

Dogfish

The smooth dogfish (also known as sand shark) that are often taken while fluke fishing are an excellent source of long, white, fleshy strip baits. Just fillet off a side of the fish, skin and slice it into strip baits.

Mackerel

Fresh mackerel is perhaps the best bait you could use for fluke fishing in the spring of the year. With mackerel making a northward trek along our coastline, and fluke making a westward inshore trek each spring, they are bound to be on a collision course. Mackerel-tipped bucktails or plain mackerel strips on either a tandem or Ryder rig are both excellent choices for tempting fluke.

There are three ways in which to obtain strip baits from a fresh mackerel. With the first method, fillet each side of the fish and then cut each fillet into three long strips. One mackerel should produce six long strips of bait. The second method, which produces shorter but many more strips, is nothing more than cutting the sides of the mackerel into diagonal strips starting at the top of the fish and ending in the belly section. It's then just a matter of peeling off a strip of mackerel which should consist of a length of skin and some mackerel flesh. Whether you use the first or second method, be sure that each strip doesn't contain too much meat. I'd suggest that you trim away all excess flesh, leaving only a thin sliver of meat attached to the skin. This will allow the bait to flutter in the water.

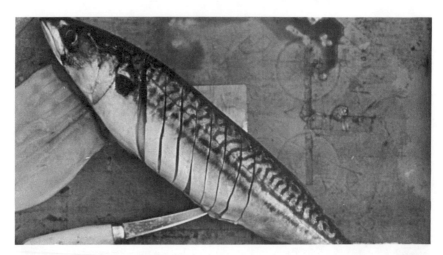

Mackerel work best in the early run in the spring and can be cut up into strips as shown.

Perhaps the most hardy mackerel bait is that which is cut from the fish's white belly area. The belly bait can be refrozen several times, and because of its firm consistency, it should serve as a good bait for several trips. To obtain this bait, cut open the mackerel's belly cavity with one stroke of a sharp knife and clean out the entrails. Lay each flap or section of the white belly area on a board and cut long strips from this area. You should get two to four strips from each white side of the stomach cavity. Be sure that the belly strips are tapered, with no ragged edges.

Small tinker mackerel four to seven inches long are excellent fluke baits when used whole. Unfortunately, it is almost impossible for the angler to obtain a supply of this bait except for those occasions in late summer when they are mixed in with the snappers. If the angler does catch tinker mackerel in any quantity, they may be frozen whole for fluking. The skin and bones will keep the fish sufficiently intact and effective. Whole tinker mackerel must be rigged with tandem hook arrangement. The top hook should be passed through the bottom lip and out the top lip to keep the mouth from opening. The stinger hook should be embedded lightly through the skin behind the second dorsal fin. Under no circumstances should a live mackerel be fished on the bottom for fluke as they will quickly entangle any terminal tackle.

Some anglers prefer to cut only the belly of the mackerel into strips since it is tougher and stays on the hook longer.

70

Strip baits from fluke, sea robin, dogfish and small blues are all excellent choices to fool big fluke.

Sea Robin

The sea robin also yields excellent strip baits for fluke, particularly the doormat variety. Sea robins often are found in the same areas as feeding fluke, providing both a means of locating them and an effective bait supply at the same time. The tough skin of the sea robin makes it virtually impossible to be stolen by an attacking fluke, but it can be aggravating for the angler trying to remove a mangled piece of bait from the hook for replacement. Use a knife. Whole sea robins may be frozen for future use and still retain their effectiveness.

To cut a sea robin into strip baits, lift the pectoral fin and make a vertical cut from the dorsal fin to mid-belly. Put the blade of the knife in the cut and turn it flat, then slice off the entire side of the fish with a slow, sawing motion while holding the flesh down with the palm of your hand. Lay the side of the sea robin skin-down on a flat surface. Running in a straight line down the center of the flesh is a series of small bones. Cut alongside them down to the skin from the wide end of the fillet to the tapered portion. Then cut the skin with a series of long, sweeping strokes of the blade — *DO NOT* use a sawing motion. If the sea robin is large, allowing strip baits more than an inch of thickness, it will be necessary to turn the strip on its side and trim off the excess flesh. One sea robin will yield four strip baits.

Special care should be taken when rigging strips of sea robin on a tandem hook so that it will move through the water naturally. The point of the top hook should be embedded through the skin first then out the flesh. The stinger hook should be within two inches of the point of the taper, but offset from the center of the strip to allow for easier hook penetration. The bend of the hook should not be completely encumbered with the flesh of the strip bait. The entire hook point and barb must be exposed.

This young angler used a strip bait to take a big fluke home for dinner.

Winter Flounder

If you think I'm confusing a winter flounder with a summer fluke, let me put your mind at ease. During the summer months, small baby winter flounder inhabit most of the tidal rivers and shallow bays of their range as they gain weight and size during their initial growth year. These baby winter flounders are fed upon by the resident fluke population.

A survey taken in Long Island waters a few years back showed that 30% of all fluke sampled had bay winter flounders in their stomachs. Since no tackle stores stock winter flounders as bait, you have to seine them using a two-man net. Your netting efforts should be in shallow water where the bottom consists of a combination of mud and sand. If you're fortunate enough to net some baby flounders, place them into a cooler of salt water that has an aerating pump installed.

When you've reached the fluke grounds, hook the flounder lightly through the back skin, avoiding the backbone. Since baby winter flounder tend to be on the small side, you should use smaller and lighter hooks. Most anglers employing this method use freshwater hooks in the 4 - 6 size. Also, since the flounder are fragile, you don't want them to tire by dragging around a heavy hook. This is where fishing with the previously-mentioned fish-finder rig comes in handy. It's somewhat of a hassle obtaining this bait, but once you've seen how effective it is for catching fluke, you'll certainly consider using tiny flounders when available.

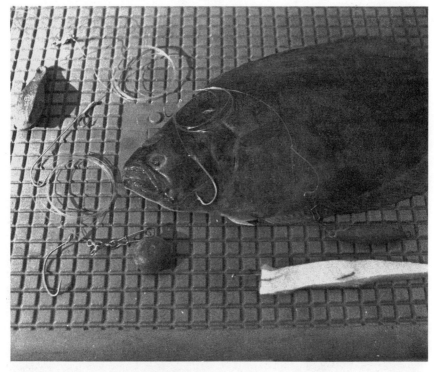

The well prepared summer flounder fishermen uses a variety of rigs and baits to adapt to each day's changing fishing conditions.

6
LOCATING FLUKE

As with most bottom feeding-fish, knowing how to locate fluke is half the battle of catching them. In order to find and catch fluke consistently, the angler must be familiar with the types of bottom formations and composition that they frequent. He must also understand how the tides and currents will dictate when a certain bottom formation will be inhabited. Once a productive bottom formation has been located, you must also know how to "mark" it so that the area can be found on subsequent fishing trips. The angler who understands and masters these techniques will see his catch become two or three times that of a fisherman who drifts aimlessly and only takes an occassional fluke.

There is an old adage in the real estate business that says the three most important words in buying property are *LOCATION — LOCATION — LOCATION.* The same adage is also true for fluke fishing. You don't want to waste your time and efforts in areas that do not have the potential of holding fluke. Perhaps only 10 - 20% of the water in your fluke fishing territory contains fluke. This rather small area is where you should be fishing, avoiding the remaining larger, unproductive places.

Of course, finding the best location to fish is the trick to good fishing. Like most fish, fluke move with the ebb and flow of the tides, but they don't travel helter skelter all over a bay or river. They follow the edges of channels or other bottom structure for security and a good supply of food. Find these traveling routes that fluke use as the tides rise and fall and you will experience better fishing.

Let's see how tides, currents and the many different types of bottom structure affect fluke fishing.

Tides and Currents

As with most predatory game fish, the tidal and current movements of the water play an extremely important role in the fluke's feeding habits. But in order to understand why, you must first have a working knowledge of how the tides and currents function. This can be confusing, even for anglers with many years of experience. The subject deserves a few words of clarification.

Tides are the vertical movement of water. There are two stages of the tide — high tide and low tide — approximately six hours apart, giving us four tides a day — two high and two low. The water will pause for a short time as the tide changes — this is known as slack water or change of the tide. High tide tables that give the times of high tide in various locations for a particular day are printed in The Fisherman and the sports section of most daily newspapers. But these times will only tell you when the water will reach its highest level. What interests the fluke fisherman is the time that the water will slacken as it prepares to move in the opposite direction. This is when currents come into play.

The current is the horizontal movement of water. There are two basic movements — incoming (or flood) and outgoing (ebb). Each has the same duration as the tides — approximately six hours. The high tide occurs during incoming water and low tide takes place during the outgoing. The high tide tables give the time when the water reaches its highest level, not when the currents stop and start at the slack. This is where many anglers go wrong. Let's look at a hypothetical example to see why this is so important.

Let's say there is a slack tide at 8 a.m. in an inlet. The incoming current then begins to move, bringing water through the inlet and into the bay. After the current has been moving for two hours, the water in the inlet will reach its highest level, and this is the time (10 a.m.) that will be given in the tables for high tide in the area. *BUT THE WATER WILL CONTINUE TO MOVE FOR AN ADDITIONAL FOUR HOURS BEFORE SLACKING.* Although the water in the inlet itself has reached its highest level, the areas beyond it have not. The current must therefore continue to carry water to these areas until they have also attained their highest level.

There isn't any set time difference between when the water will reach its highest level (high tide) and when the current will slack before changing direction. The difference may be ten minutes, six hours or anywhere in between. How do you know what the time difference will be for a particular area? Start by computing the high tide from the tide tables for the area you are going to fish. This time will be the starting point for further calculations. When you are on the water, note the time that the water actually goes slack just before the incoming current starts. Compare this time to the time for high tide and note the difference. Is it one hour? Two? Two-and-a-half? Whatever the time difference is, subtract it from the time for high tide and you will have the approximate time that incoming water begins in that area in relationship to the high tide. In the example we have been using, the time difference was two hours, so the angler would subtract this from the time given for high tide to find out when the incoming current begins in the inlet.

The reason why currents are so important to successful fluke fishing is that the fluke use them as an aid when feeding. When moving water comes into contact with a bottom formation, a turbulence is created. This turbulence will vary in intensity and duration during different stages of the current, so certain times on a particular bottom formation will be more productive than others. For example, a sand bar in the inlet we have been discussing may only be a productive area for fluke during the first two hours of the incoming tide. This is important to know, obviously. Why spend six hours of fishing there if only two are productive? After you know the productive current stages for several locations you can have a full six hours of good fishing by moving to each bottom formation at its prime productively. Naturally, this technique will be reflected in the size of your catch.

Bottom Formations

A working knowledge of bottom formations is probably the most important information that an angler can possess for successful fluke fishing. While fluke can be taken over a flat, uniform bottom, it will be slow fishing because the fish will be spread over a wide area. But fluke will congregate in numbers around many types of bottom formations because of the food they find there.

The reasons that bottom formations attract fluke are usually two-fold: because of their shape and location, as the current passes over them a turbulence is created that disrupts the movement of baitfish. Formations also usually provide a good bottom composition or other factors that make it easy for fluke to camouflage themselves so that they may strike from ambush. In either case, find a bottom formation with a population of baitfish and you more than likely have located a good number of fluke.

Bottom formations can be located both visually and with the aid of electronic depth recorders. A change in water color or turbulence on the water's surface will often tip the angler to a bottom formation below. But the best means of locating them is with a depth recorder that tells the angler of any changes in depth, which is what a bottom formation is.

An excellent way of finding these changes in bottom formations is through the use of aerial photography. To obtain good color pictures of your favorite fishing holes, use a 35mm camera equipped with a wide angle lens. Set your shutter speed to 1/500 of a second and your ASA to 120 even though the color slide film you're using has an ASA rating of 64. Don't shoot your pictures through either the windshield or side windows of the aircraft as this causes reflections. It's best to open the window before taking pictures. Plan your flight on a day with minimal wind, plenty of sun, and be sure to schedule your trip in a high wing aircraft to coincide with the ebb tide of the area you're photographing. The resulting underwater secrets which should be revealed by the photos will be extraordinary.

By concentrating your angling efforts at major bottom formations, you'll increase your fluke-caught-per-trip ratio.

Channels

Channels are perhaps the easiest places in which to fish for fluke especially in bay waters. A channel is defined as deep trough flanked by shallow water. The only problem with fishing channels is that they are usually crowded with anglers trolling for fluke, drifting for fluke, bucktailing for fluke and, invariably, there is a boat or two anchored in the middle of all this boating traffic, making a traffic jam inevitable. In addition to the many anglers fishing channel areas, these same channels act as thoroughfares for high-powered boats heading in and out of the various inlets at seemingly their only speed . . . full-throttle. There can be a lot of wave action and boating noise during the mid-morning and late afternoon in channel areas.

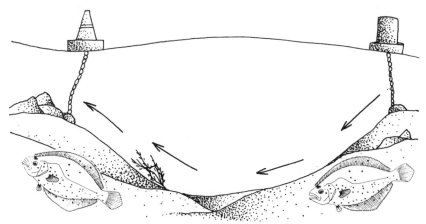

However, during the weekdays and early and late in the day when the channel areas are quiet, they can be very productive for fluke. Channels are extremely easy to fish and locate because of the many black and red numbered buoys that serve as navigational aids to mark their outside perimeters. These buoys are usually placed five to seven feet offshore of where the shallow water drops-off into the deep waters of the channel. It is along these structure breaks that most fluke are caught as opposed to down the middle of the channel.

Knowing whether the tide is rising or falling makes a difference in how you fish a channel area. When the tide is incoming and the water is rising, baitfish and fluke will migrate out of the deepest parts of the channel and towards the shallower water of the flats. This is when they are moving up the slope of the channel edge, so you should be fishing inshore of the marker buoys. When the tide is outgoing of falling, the reverse is true, with the fish moving down the channel edges towards the deeper areas of the channel. This is when you should be fishing parallel with the buoys or offshore of the buoy pattern.

Slopes

Remember the motto: *Inshore of the buoys on Incoming . . . Offshore of the buoys when Outgoing.* Most people putting together good scores of fluke will either troll or drift along the length of the channel edges. Don't fish for fluke across the channel, but rather along its length . . . and whenever you see a channel become narrow or enter a bend, you can bet your last thin dime that there are fluke in this area.

A slope is simply a gradual slant of the bottom as the depth increases. In deep water, the fluke will lie facing the direction of the current, which is usually parallel with the slope. The baitfish will usually swim with the current along the length of the slope.

Let's suppose that there is a slope in the ocean where the depth of the water gradually increases from 40 to 70 feet. The fluke will usually congregate at one or two depths: more often than not they will be most numerous at the top of the slope where the bottom begins to drop from 40 feet. A smaller number of fish will be found at the bottom of the slope where the water begins

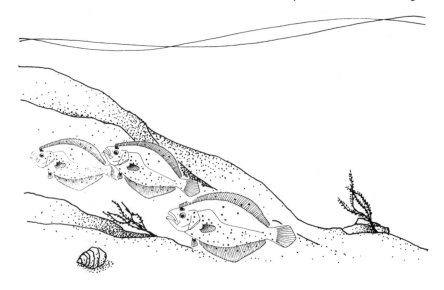

a constant depth of 70 feet. But it is interesting to note that if there are any doormats in the area, they will usually be found at the bottom of the slope for some reason. Fluke will also be found on the slant of the slope itself, but will usually be scattered.

Very little water turbulence is found around a gradual slope, so visual location is usually not practical if it is in deep water, making a depth recorder essential for locating these "sunken" slopes. But if the slope is in shallow water, it may often be located visually simply by being alert for a change in the color or darkness of the water. This condition usually occurs most prominently close to a shoreline.

The same fluke movement patterns as described for channels also apply when underwater slopes are located in shallow water. Since fluke are predators, they will follow forage fish as they swim inshore as the tide is rising and then offshore as the tide is falling, so keep this pattern in mind.

Tidal Rips

Tidal rips usually occur where two opposing currents come into contact with each other. This creates a turbulence as the waters intermingle. Any turbulence slows down baitfish. The fluke will lie either directly in this turbulence or to one side of it, but never too far away.

Tidal rips are easy for the angler to locate, particularly when the wind and seas are calm. The rip will appear on the surface where the currents meet and looks just like its name implies: a "rip" in the surface of the water. When a tidal rip has been located, it is always a good idea to drop a buoy directly on it in case conditions change. If the wind increases or changes direction and the water begins to pick up, it will be difficult or impossible to pick out the rip visually from the rest of the choppy water.

Inlets

Inlets from the ocean to a bay or harbor are excellent areas for fluke fishing for a variety of reasons. All water that moves in and out of the inland body of water must pass through the inlet, which creates strong currents due to the funneling effect as the mass of water is squeezed through the narrow opening. An outgoing tide is particularly productive because it has a flushing effect, carrying small baitfish and other food through the neck of the opening. Fluke will frequent the inlet during the outgoing tide when there is an abundance of prey caught in the swift current — an easy meal to feast on.

Inlets are particularly effective in late summer. As they move out of their summer haunts in the shallow water of a bay or harbor, the fluke will tend to bunch up in an inlet and remain there for several weeks, fattening up on baitfish in preparation for their offshore migration. The best areas to fish in an inlet are along the edges around the channel markers and near the sand shoals that often build up in the mouth. Also look for small pockets and depressions around eddies.

In many cases, offshore several miles from most inlets, there are a series of shallow water crowns or ridges which are nothing more than some high bottom surrounded by deeper water. During the fall, as the fluke leave the various inlets, they will pause for a week or two at these crowns to feed on sand eels and spearing before they venture further offshore towards the continental shelf. If the fall fishing begins to taper off at your respective inlet, find the nearest crown to the inlet on a navigation chart, and make that the target of your next fluke trip. Chances are, you'll hit the fluke jackpot right on the nose and encounter some exciting fishing.

Flats

Flats are very shallow areas in bay waters and are usually inaccessible to all boats except those with shallow draft. Fluke will often forage for small baitfish, crabs and shrimp that are found in these shallow waters and, as a rule, you'll tend to find them where there are small depressions and structure breaks in the sand. Remember that sand flats are not as "flat" as your kitchen table top, and within each sand flat there may be several tidal pools, small ridges and bars.

The same bottom type structure that is found in deeper waters are also found on the sand flats but in miniature size. The best way to locate these structures variances on the flats is to troll these areas at low tide if possible. Trolling allows you to cover a substantial amount of ground and when the tide is low, potholes, ridges, pools and tidal cuts through the water gushes are all visible. All you have to do is to mark these spots on a map and remember their location the next time you fish these areas.

Wading the flats in a pair of knee boots or old sneakers and casting with a flyrod is an excellent way of locating structure breaks from the ground level for future reference. It's also a pleasant way to enjoy some cool fishing on a hot summer afternoon. Just be sure that you keep a wary eye on the tidal phase, as you don't want to become stranded from your boat with an incoming tide. If your boat is too big to troll the flats, fish where the depth of the water begins to increase along the edges of the flat. The fluke will often line up along the down-current edge of a flat, facing the shallow water, feeding on whatever baitfish are swept off by the moving current. Don't waste time fishing along the up-current edge of a flat or, for that matter, on any bottom structure where few fluke will be found.

Shoals

A shoal is a large mound usually composed of sand, that has been built up by tidal and current movements and rises from the bottom like a small hill. They may be located visually by the surface rips on the water above them created by water turbulence, or by cruising an area with either a flasher or graph depth sounder and searching for rapid fluctuations in depth. Large shoal formations are also shown on nautical charts.

Large shoals are probably the most productive bottom formation for fluke because of the tremendous water turbulence often found there. Study the diagram to see how this turbulence is created.

Schools of baitfish always travel in the same direction as a moving current because it is the course of least resistance. When they come into contact with this large shoal and its accompanying water turbulence they are tossed and turned. The fluke instinctively know this and will lie along the up-current (right) side fo the shoal, gobbling up all the helpless baitfish that come within range. Some fluke will also be at the top of the shoal, and a few will take position on the down-current (left) side of the shoal. As a rule, the larger fluke in the doormat class will be found on the down-current slope where there is less competition from smaller fluke, which will be concentrated most heavily on the up-current side.

Most shoals will be productive during both currents — incoming and outgoing. When the current slackens, the fluke will simply swim over the top of the shoal to the other side so that they will again be facing up-current when the tide changes direction. So, when the current slackens around a shoal, the fishing will experience a lull because there won't be any water turbulence from the still waters and the fish are on the move to another area with more turbulence.

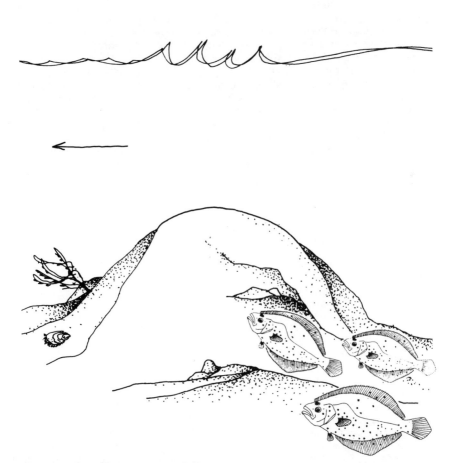

Beach Drop-Offs

The point where the water depth drops suddenly next to a beach is a prime fluking area for many reasons. Most importantly, baitfish will congregate en masse on the shallow shelf between the surf line and the drop-off. The high water clarity in these shallows over a sandy bottom gives the baitfish a degree of protection against the fluke and other predators that strike from ambush. The fluke will lie right on the edge of the drop-off and face the shallow water, patiently waiting for small baitfish that may become careless and venture too near.

Beach drop-offs are also very easy for the angler to locate visually without the aid of a recorder. The shallow shelf and drop-off will be distinctly marked by a sudden darkening of the water, almost as if a line has been drawn. Concentrate your fishing along this color line and you're in business. Unfortunately, the fish found in these areas are usually in the smaller end of the size range. But, on the other hand, fluke fishing on slopes as a rule is usually not affected adversely by changes in current direction because productivity doesn't rely upon water turbulence.

If the water clarity is such that you cannot see a discernible change in its color when it drops from shallow water to deeper water, and you don't have a depth recorder on board, try fishing between a pair of hopscotched marker buoys. To do this, find an initial beach drop-off by heading your boat towards the beach with your fishing line straight up and down (90°). When the angle of the line entering the water begins to decrease (with the same length of line extended), you are entering shallow water. At this point, drop off your first marker buoy. Repeat this same exercise several hundred yards up or down the beach, depending on boating traffic, and you'll wind up having two points of fishing reference that mark beach drop-offs. It's now just a matter of trolling back and forth between the two markers until you run out of fish. When this occurs, pick up your lower marker and place it several hundred yards above the upper marker, using the same line-angle technique described above. When this is accomplished, you've now established two new reference points between which you should troll. I'm suggesting that you troll between the reference points instead of drifting as, in most cases, either the wind or the tide will not allow you to drift from one marker to another and, if you're not on the structure break, you might as well keep your baits in the boat as you won't be catching many fluke. You can continue to hopscotch your marker buoys up the beach until you either have filled your cooler or run out of beachfront trolling space.

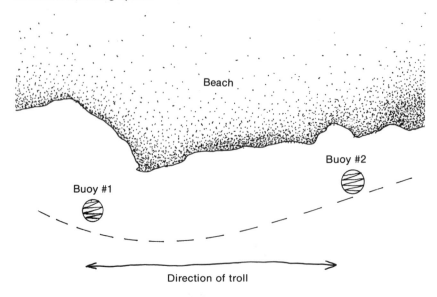

Beach

Buoy #2

Buoy #1

Direction of troll

Wrecks

Sunken wrecks are excellent places to find fluke, particularly the larger variety, because of the "oasis" effect of the wreck. If surrounded by a relatively flat bottom, marine life of all types will be attracted to the protection that the wreck will afford. Small marine growths will anchor themselves to the hull, which will attract small fish that feed upon them which, in turn, will attract predators such as fluke, completing the food chain.

Large fluke will most often be found on the flat bottom all around the fringes of a wreck. They usually won't be found on the hull itself, which has a minimum of the flat surface that the fluke can utilize. Stages of tidal movements will usually not affect a wreck's productivity, which is a marked advantage over many other types of bottom formations. Ocean wrecks are particularly productive for large doormats in late summer and early fall when fluke make their offshore migration.

The general location of many wrecks may be discovered by consulting nautical charts, then scouting the area with a depth recorder. But it should be noted that charts usually only show that small percentage of wrecks that are near enough to the surface to pose a possible danger to navigation. So, how do you find those that aren't on the chart? By paying your dues and spending many hours searching blindly for wrecks by trial and error. Don't look for anyone to take you by the hand and show them to you . . . the location of a "virgin" wreck is probably one of the best-kept secrets in the sport of fishing.

Points of Land

A sand bar will often build up around a point of land jutting into the water. As the moving current changes course and swings around a point of land, sand is often deposited and a sand bar is built up over a period of time. They are easy to locate visually by the light shade of the shallow water over the sand, or by consulting nautical charts and looking for areas similar to the one shown in the diagram.

Fluke are attracted to a point of land because of the water turbulence. When moving current meets the point shown in the diagram, the main volume of water will swing outward and run along the edge of the point, then swing back to its orginal course after passing the tip of the formation. Some of the water will wash over the top of the bar itself with little change in direction.

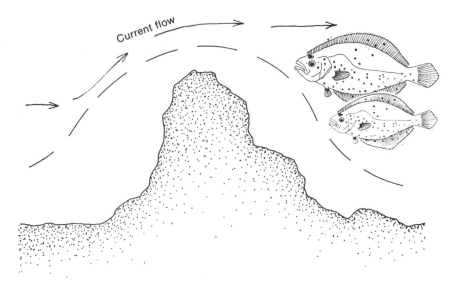

This movement of the current creates an unusual drifting pattern, because a drifting boat will follow the same course as the moving body of water. As a rule, fluke would be dispersed around this sand bar as follows: a few fish will be strung out along the up-current edge of the sand bar, where the water depth is about to change from 18 to 3 feet. A fairly large concentration of fluke will be at the end of the bar where the water changes direction to swing around the tip. The greatest concentration of fish will be found on the down-current edge of the point, where the fluke will line up shoulder to shoulder facing the shallow water and feed on the baitfish being swept over the top of the sand bar.

Curiously, the vast majority of anglers will never drift over the prime down-current edge of a sand bar. They will usually position their boat on the up-current side in 18 feet of water and start their drift. But the boat will move in the same direction as the large arrows, creating a drift along the up-current edge of the bar. You will pick up a few fluke with this drift, particularly as the boat swings around the tip of the bar, but you will never get near the greatest concentration of fish lying along the down-current edge.

So, where do you begin a drift under these conditions? Position the boat on top of the sand bar itself in three feet of water. By starting a drift there, you *MUST* pass over the down-current edge and its concentration of fish. As soon as the depth of the water begins to drop from three to 18 feet, you should hook up with a fish. This is also an excellent area to troll.

Sand Bars

In addition to the sand bars that are formed on the down-tide side of a point of land, other types of sand bars are formed between two separate channels, adjacent to sand flats, in the middle of inlets, and where side channels and creeks enter a larger bay or river. While these sand bars tend to be different in shape, they all have one thing in common. They all produce large quantities of fluke, if they are fished on the down-tide side of the bar on an outgoing tide.

Sand bars often hold a myriad of forage fish, plus crabs and shrimp. When

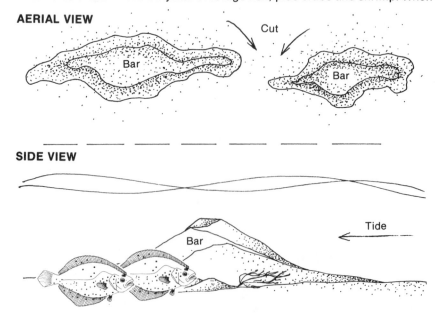

AERIAL VIEW

Cut

Bar

Bar

SIDE VIEW

Tide

Bar

the outgoing tide begins to flow over these bars, the baitfish are flushed down-tide and, as the tide continues to ebb, the crests of the bars begin to stick above the surface. Since the baitfish need water to exist, they naturally flow along with the tide towards the pocket of fluke that have set up residency on the down-tide side of the bar. It is not unusual to catch upwards of 50 fluke down-tide of a bar that is no more than a few acres in size.

Trolling rather than drifting is the suggested method for fishing a sand bar. With this method, you can control both the direction and speed of your boat and bait as opposed to being at the mercy of the tide and wind. This is a good place to use the hi-low rig and a pair of killies. Often, a sand bar will split in half and where once water flowed over the entire bar on the outgoing tide, it now flows through the cut between the two bars. When you encounter such a situation, be sure to fish the mouth of the bar cut. If the length of the cut's opening is rather small, making trolling impractical, try anchoring up-tide of the cut between the two sand bars and begin casting bait-tipped bucktails down-tide of the cut. Retrieve your bucktail in short hops along the bottom, making sure it passes through where the water is flowing through the cut. This is, without doubt, one of the most productive spots for fluke.

Reefs

Reefs are large humps or plateaus that rise from the ocean floor with a relatively flat bottom surrounding them. They have the same "oasis" effect as a wreck, but reefs are usually considerably larger and their productivity will often be more affected by stages of the tidal currents.

As with the wreck, fluke will be found along the edge of a reef, particularly if it is a gradual slope. They will congregate most heavily along the down-current edge, feeding on the baitfish that have been carried over the formation by the moving current. When the current changes direction, the fluke will simply move to the edge that then becomes the down-current side of the reef. As a rule, any fluke on the top portion of a reef will be scattered as there isn't any incentive for them to congregate.

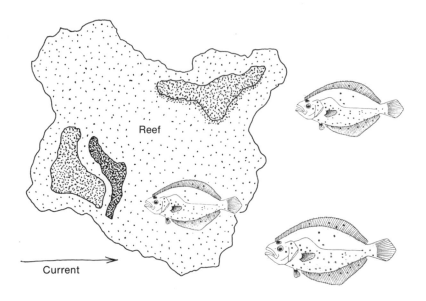

Reef

Current

Depressions

A depression is a shallow hole with a uniform water depth surrounding it. Small pods of fluke will often be found in such a depression because it may contain calm water even if there is a moving current directly overhead. Baitfish seek out a depression for this reason and use it as a rest area. The fluke will also lie in a hole to attack baitfish passing over it as they are carried along by the current.

It is easiest to locate depressions with a depth sounder, but they may be located visually in shallow water by looking for a patch of dark water. Once located, don't waste too much time fishing over a depression if you don't get action right away or the fishing suddenly dies after two or three fish, because they usually won't hold too many fluke at one time. So, when the action dies, look for another depression or bottom formation to fish.

Since most depressions aren't very large in length, they are difficult to either drift or troll across as your bait is only over the depressions for a few seconds. Rather than drifting or trolling, I'd suggest that you anchor your boat up-tide of the depression and then cast a weighted bucktail past the hole and begin a slow retrieve of the lure through the hole. The fluke will interpret the bucktail as being a baitfish intruder. At this point, no self-respecting fluke will let this easy meal escape and should provide you with a jolting strike.

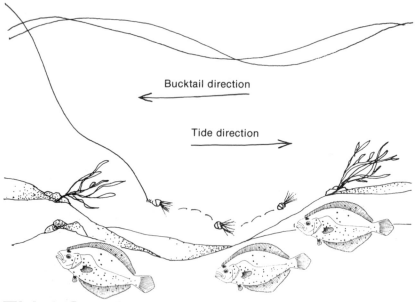

Bucktail direction

Tide direction

Tidal Creeks

There are two basic types of tidal creeks that empty into a bay or harbor. The first type is where a freshwater creek enters the bay. Between the fresh and saltwater areas, a section of "brackish" water develops which is a combination of the two water types. Marine plant life flourishes here in brackish water, as do many species of bivalves and crustaceans which, in turn, are a source of food and attraction for the small baitfish that fluke feed upon. The second type of tidal creek is located along the coastline salt marshes, and fills up entirely with salt water as the tide rises to fill the low-lying wetlands.

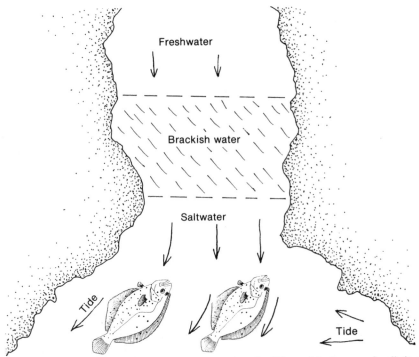

Freshwater

Brackish water

Saltwater

Tide

Tide

While the type of water in these two creeks is different in terms of salinity, they both have two things in common. Both harbor large concentrations of baitfish on the incoming tide, and when the tide begins to recede the mouths of these creeks become populated with fluke waiting for an easy meal. It's like waiting at the end of a gum drop assembly line with your mouth open. All you have to do is lie there and the treats will come to you.

The water leaving the tidal creek is soon influenced by the tidal currents of the bay or harbor it is entering. Therefore, most fluke will be located on the down-tide side of the tidal creek's mouth, especially during the first hour of the outgoing tide. Since tidal creeks are usually narrow, the only practical way to fish these areas is to anchor near the mouth and cast bucktails and saltwater flies to these fluke-rich areas. The bucktail or fly should be cast into the mouth of the creek and be allowed to drift along with the tide, just as a natural baitfish. A moving boat that is either trolled or drifted near the creeks mouth will often spook a pocket of fluke into deeper surrounding waters, so anchoring is an advantage here.

Jetties

Since many members of the fluke fishing fraternity do not use boats, they are left to seek this species from land-based points of operation. This, however, is not too much of a handicap as fluke fishing from the jetties that dot our coastline can be very productive at times. Two important things, however, should be remembered when fluke fishing from a jetty. First, the most productive time to fish jetties for fluke is during the last two hours of incoming tide and the last two hours of outgoing. It is during these four hours of tide that the fluke will have moved inshore following the baitfish that travel along the outside edge of the surf line. This time frame also puts fluke into relatively easy casting range of the jetty-based angler.

These boat anglers are netting a fluke they caught while drifting a short distance off a jetty.

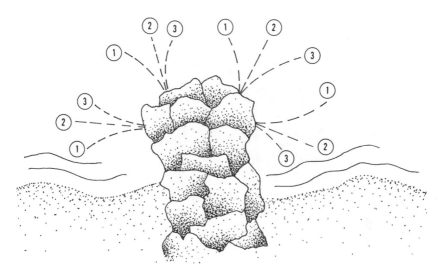

The second important prerequisite when fishing for fluke from a jetty is that bait must be kept moving by slowly retrieving it along the bottom to produce any substantial quantities of fish. If you let your bait just sit there in one spot too long, it will inevitably become a snack for the local crab population. With casting and retrieving a necessity, long, fluttering strip baits are the suggested menu. Strips of squid, mackerel, fluke belly or sand sharks make ideal baits. The outer two-thirds of most jetties is probably the most productive area. An easy way to pinpoint a pocket of fluke is to fan cast. If there are no takers, move out another 15 feet and fan cast again. If you do catch a fluke from a jetty, cast again to that same spot as you may have found a small pocket of fish. I've seen jetty anglers take up to 20 nice-sized fluke by casting to a specific area, while other anglers fishing close by went fishless. If you've completely fan-casted an entire jetty and still have come up with an empty bucket, move on to the next jetty along the beachfront and perhaps you'll hit the flatfish jackpot. Remember the importance of wearing cleated rubbers while fishing slippery jetties.

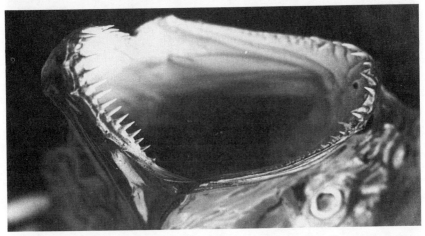

The last thing a killie sees when attacked by a summer flounder! Predators, Fluke lie near jetties waiting to pounce on unsuspecting baitfish.

89

7
DRIFTING FOR FLUKE

Now that you know from Chapter Six that most fluke are located along channel edges, slopes, tidal rips, inlets, shoals, beach drop-offs, points of land, sand bars, reefs and depressions, what would be the best way to fish these varied spots from a boat? Basically, there are only two major ways to fish for fluke at these different bottom formations: you can either troll under motor power or you can drift these formations using the wind and the current as your means of movement. What determines which method you use depends on the weather conditions, specifics of the actual formation you're fishing and your boat size. Let's look at some different strategies.

The primary fishing method for catching fluke is drifting, which is simply allowing the boat to be moved through the water by the forces of the wind and current. It is an extremely effective method of taking fish, but there is more expertise involved than may first meet the eye. The primary purpose of drifting is to present the bait to a fluke in a natural manner — moving in the same direction and at the same speed as a baitfish. Drifting has the added advantage of covering a wide area of the bottom, bringing up the angler to the fish, rather than anchoring and waiting for the fluke to stumble across the bait.

Drifting is a very pleasant way to fish, especially on a warm sunny day. However, don't get lulled by the friendly sun. It is critical to good catches of fluke that the drift be adjusted and fine tuned so the boat takes the angler, and the baits, over the most productive bottom structure. Drifting aimlessly over a wide flat bottom devoid of structure may not catch many fish, but drifting over the right structure will put alot of good eating fish in your cooler.

Drifting Over Formations

The first order of business when drifting for fluke is to locate one of the bottom formations discussed in Chapter Six that you think has good potential. If most of your fluke fishing is confined to one area, you will quickly learn where the productive formations are and you won't have to waste time scouting around. But when fishing in an unfamiliar area, you're going to have to pay your dues and spend some time learning it — a *LONG* time.

The best method of locating a bottom formation is to slowly cruise around an area with one eyeball focused on either a flasher or graph recorder. For a starting point, it's a good idea to consult a nautical chart for the area to find any rapid depth changes that tip you off to a potentially productive bottom formation. It's also a good idea to visit your local bait and tackle proprietor and ask him to pinpoint the local hotspots on the chart for you.

Once a formation with good potential has been located, the next order of business is to decide where you're going to start the drift. You must first find out what direction the boat is going to drift in, because you want to start the boat in a position where the drift will carry it directly over the formation. If you can't be sure what direction the drift will take by observing the wind direction and speed and the direction the current is moving, then your best bet is to make a practice drift. It doesn't have to be that long — just let the boat settle down and notice how it drifts. Then position the boat so that the drift will carry you over the formation.

Drifting Blind

Drifting blind is simply allowing the boat to drift on its own accord without any particular goal in mind. It isn't a very effective method for taking fluke in quantity, but it does allow the angler to cover a lot of bottom. If you don't have a depth recorder or the fluke are scattered over a flat bottom, you may be forced to drift blind. But, don't despair, you may get lucky — it's not unusual to take a fluke in the doormat class with this method because they are usually "lone wolves" and don't hang out with the pack.

Drift Direction

The feeding habits of fluke have a direct bearing on the best direction for a drift. Fluke are predators, feeding on almost any baitfish they can capture. To be successful, fluke must know the habits of the baitfish they feed on. All baitfish have one habit in common — they will tend to swim down-current, in the same direction as the moving water. The only reason that a baitfish will swim up-current is because something has spooked it. So, it's a safe bet that a fluke has seldom observed a baitfish swimming up-current naturally, but when he does, he tends to make a quick meal of this struggling morsel (but more of this in the trolling section). Fluke will, therefore, tend to facing up-current watching both forward and to the side somewhat for baitfish that are swimming towards them. However, keep in mind that while you may be drifting with the current, unless you're over the productive bottom formations previously mentioned, you're probably not presenting baits to any fluke.

The speed at which the boat is drifting is the second most important factor to contend with. A drift that is too slow or almost stationary won't trigger the predatory instincts of the fluke. The boat also won't cover much distance, so valuable time may be wasted by fishing over a poor bottom composition. On the other hand, if the drift is too fast you will also be at a disadvantage. It will be hard to keep the rig on the bottom in the feeding zone without using excessive sinker weight. If the fluke are eating heartily, they may not have the desire to waste energy pursuing a baitfish that is moving faster than the rest of the food supply. And if the fish are in a narrow band your bait may pass through it before a fluke has a chance to spot the bait and pursue it.

The speed and direction of a drift will be determined by three factors: type of boat, prevailing wind conditions and the direction of the current.

Boat Design

The design of its hull will greatly affect how a boat will drift. As a rule, the more boat in the water, the greater the water-resistance created — which is desirable, because the current will be the predominant factor and move the boat in the same direction as the moving current under moderate wind conditions.

A deep-V or cathedral hull is the first choice for fluke fishing; a modified-V is second choice, and a flat bottom boat third. The weight of a boat is also an important factor as to how much of the hull is submerged. Heavy wood or fiberglass boats are preferred over the light aluminum (or "tin") boats that just sit on top of the water with very little of the hull submerged. Light boats will be influenced more by the wind than current, making the wind the predominant force influencing the drift.

Boats with navy tops and canvas for shelter are best for fluke fishing, rather than those with permanent superstructures. This is because the canvas may be raised or lowered at will to suit the prevailing wind conditions. If the wind is strong and you wish to decrease its influence upon the drift, take down any canvas that will have a sail-like effect. If you want to realize the full influence of the wind, raise all the canvas.

An outboard engine can be used to increase or decrease the amount of water resistance and the influence the current will have on a drifting boat. If you want to increase the current's influence, keep the lower unit of the outboard in the water. To decrease it, simply raise the engine clear of the water to cut down on the water resistance.

As a final thought, keep in mind that the number of people and the amount of gear you place in a boat will also determine how low or how high it sits in the water and how fast it drifts with the wind and current pushing it.

Winds

Winds are a major factor in drifting because they are so variable. However, the wind direction is not as important as the *RELATION* of that direction to the way the water is flowing. A wind blowing against the tide will slow down the drift. With the wind and tide going in the same direction, the drift will be speeded up.

Currents

The direction of the current has a strong effect on the direction that a drifting boat will take. The current in a particular area will normally only flow in two directions — one when the current is incoming (flood tide) and in the opposite direction when the current is outgoing (ebb tide). The only variable factor to a current other than this speed is its speed of flow, which may vary considerably during the course of a month, depending on the relative positions of the sun and moon to each other. As a rule, the current will be running the strongest during a new moon and a little stronger than normal during a full moon. There will also be unusually high and low tides during these periods.

Types of Drift

The forces of wind and current can combine in countless variations that will influence a drifting boat. Let's look at four basic combinations and analyze their effect upon the speed and direction of a drift.

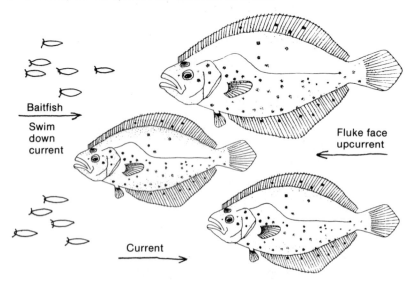

Baitfish

Swim down current

Fluke face upcurrent

Current

LIGHT BREEZE AND CURRENT IN SAME DIRECTION

These are the very best conditions for drifting for fluke. As we can see, a light breeze and the current are moving in the same direction. The breeze is just strong enough to help move the hull of a small boat in the same direction as the current at a moderate speed.

STRONG WIND AND CURRENT IN THE SAME DIRECTION

When a steady wind of 12 mph or more is blowing, you're going to have difficulties even if it is in the same direction as the current. In this case a wind of 12 to 20+ mph is blowing from east to west, the same direction as the moving water. Their forces are cumulative and combine to push the boat too fast for a good drift. Two negative results will usually occur when this situation arises: the bait will be moving too fast to interest a fluke, and you will have difficulty keeping the rig on the bottom unless you use heavier sinkers. Fishing will be only fair at best.

All is not lost, however, because there are a few actions that may be taken to minimize the force of the wind. The wind is exerting its force when it meets the resistance of a boat's surface area. So, if you want to weaken the force of the wind, you must cut down on the surface area of your boat that is exposed to it. The first move is to take down any navy tops or other canvas that has the effect of being a "sail." Then keep the bow of the boat pointed into the wind throughout the drift. You may have to keep the engine running and do a little maneuvering to accomplish this, but the effort will pay off. On small boats and skiffs the beam is usually about one-third of the length, so by pointing the bow into the wind instead of drifting broadside you are only exposing one-third of the surface area and the wind will only exert one-third of its influence. Actually, it is less than that because the side of a boat is a relatively flat surface that creates considerable resistance to wind and water, while the bow of the boat has been designed to cut through water and wind.

Drifting

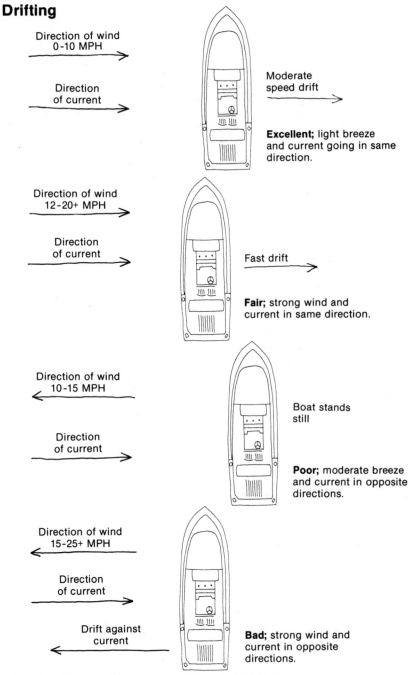

Direction of wind
0-10 MPH

Direction
of current

Moderate
speed drift

Excellent; light breeze
and current going in same
direction.

Direction of wind
12-20+ MPH

Direction
of current

Fast drift

Fair; strong wind and
current in same direction.

Direction of wind
10-15 MPH

Direction
of current

Boat stands
still

Poor; moderate breeze
and current in opposite
directions.

Direction of wind
15-25+ MPH

Direction
of current

Drift against
current

Bad; strong wind and
current in opposite
directions.

MODERATE BREEZE AND CURRENT OPPOSED

In this situation we have a moderate wind of 10 to 15 mph blowing from
east to west, opposing an east to west current. The two opposing forces are
more or less equal, cancelling each other out. So, the boat will often remain
stationary and not drift at all. The two negative results of this situation are:

the bait hasn't any natural movement and the boat isn't covering any new territory. The few fish that will be taken are those that happen to stumble over the bait on their own and are usually hungry.

Two courses of action may be taken when these conditions prevail. If you have located a small bottom formation with a population of fluke in a confined area or pocket, it is actually possible to turn the situation into an advantage. Position the boat slightly up-current of the formation so that you can "walk" the bait over it. Even though the boat may be standing still, the current is still moving, so let it help you. Lower the rig to the bottom, then keep playing out line as the current carries it over the formation. If everything suddenly stops moving, a fluke has probably grabbed the bait — wait a few moments for him to swallow it, then set the hook. If you don't hook up, reel in and repeat the "walking" technique. Another good trick is to bounce and walk an artificial such as Hopkins, diamond jig or bucktail over the bottom. Finally, you can troll the most productive spots.

STRONG WIND AND CURRENT OPPOSED

Don't waste your time when this situation arises — you just aren't going to catch many (if any) fluke when the bait is "swimming" unnaturally against the current. In this case, strong winds blowing against the direction of the current will kick up some pretty rough seas and fishing conditions will be very uncomfortable. You're pretty limited as to what you can do to reverse this situation. If you really work at it you may be able to get the boat to stand still, but why bother?

About the only thing to do is to move to a new location where the conditions will be more in your favor. For example, you can move the boat to a location near a shoreline that will allow you to fish on the lee side out of the wind. This will give you some degree of protection from its force. The higher the land mass, the more blocking effect it will have against the wind.

Another thing you can do is to move to a location where the current is flowing in a different direction. In figure 4, the strong wind is blowing from west to east against a current moving east to west. So, all you have to do is move to an area with a west to east, north to south or south to north current. Your best bet is where the current is moving crosswind (N to S, or S to N) so the wind doesn't move you too fast.

Party Boat Drifting

When fishing from a party boat, you have to rely on the knowledge and experience of the captain to put you over a productive bottom for fluke. His fishing expertise is part of the fare you pay when boarding such a vessel, but there are several things that you can do to maximize your catch of fluke on a drifting party boat. For instance, both the bow and the stern sections are probably the two most effective spots on a party boat. When fishing in these two locations, no matter which side of the boat is up-tide, you won't be hassled with the fishing line going under boat with 40 other patrons' lines.

There are times when a party boat cannot drift because of the lack of wind, and the large number of patrons on board makes trolling impossible. When this doldrum situation occurs, I'd suggest that you get a spot in the bow of the boat and flip-cast your baited hook (underhand) away from the boat. After your bait and sinker has hit bottom, begin a slow retrieve to keep your bait moving along the bottom as if the boat were drifting. Another benefit of casting with a spinning rod from a party boat is that your bait will often be the first to reach a pocket of fluke, and you could have several nice-sized fish in the bucket before the boat drifts over this hotspot. Spinning rods in the 7½ - 8-foot class makes fishing in this manner a cinch.

Multiple Drifts

When drifting for fluke, your bait probably has an effective fish-enticing corridor along the bottom of 6 - 8 feet in width. In other words, fluke can be lying 2 - 3 feet to the right or left of the bait and yet, with a burst of speed, grab a bait that is being dragged along the bottom. When you're making repeated multiple drifts over an area, you should keep two points in mind: first, don't have all your fishing rods bunched together along the gunwale. Spread them out so that their fish-enticing corridors cover a wider swath. Secondly, adjust your drift's starting point to the left or right slightly if you don't happen to pick up a fluke on a certain drift, but be sure that you remain over potential productive bottom structure.

Okay, so you've done everything right to this point and have just caught a fluke. You are using a prime bait, have located a bottom formation with a population of fluke and have a drift with good speed and direction. Now, what are you going to do? Go back and make another drift over the same area, naturally. It sounds easy, doesn't it. Well, it's not . . . unless you know what you're doing.

Out of necessity, fluke are often found in waters devoid of any reference markers. This is unfortunate, because think of how easy it would be to fish on land — "We caught that fluke at 126 Oak Street" or "in front of the fire hydrant" or "on the corner of Elm and Maple." But the fisherman doesn't have the luxury of such stationary reference points to pinpoint the exact location where a fish was taken. The boat is moving as it drifts — the exact direction and distance traveled is unknown to the angler. At the end of a drift when he looks back all the fisherman will see is a body of water that usually all looks the same — wet and green.

In order to be a successful fluke fisherman, the angler must know how to make multiple drifts over a productive area. There are two primary techniques for accomplishing this: using marker buoys and taking shore ranges.

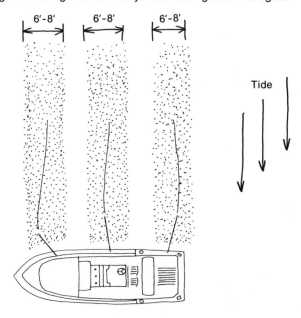

Fish Corridors

Marker Buoys

A marker buoy is simply a float attached to a weight with a length of line that the angler puts into the water for a stationary reference point. A simple marker buoy is usually more than sufficient to do the job under normal conditions.

To understand why the use of marker buoys is such a necessity to successful fluking, study the accompanying illustrations which are aerial views of a drifting boat. A broken line denotes the path of the boat while drifting and a solid line while under power. In Figure 1 we have a very common situation. The horizontal wavy line denotes a long rip on the surface of the water created by a large shoal — an excellent location for fluke. The angler wants to try to drift over it, so he positions the boat at point A. There is only a light breeze blowing, so the boat drifts in the same direction as the current. This results in the boat drifting across the rip at an angle in the path of the broken line B.

This is all well and good, as long as the angler knows it. But look at Figure 2 and see what happens when you don't know. Let's suppose that a fluke or two is taken just as the boat drifts through the rip, so when the end of the drift is reached (point B) you decide to make the same drift again. There is a natural tendency to move the boat under power across the rip at its closet point, following a course to point C, where you stop to start another drift — the same as the successful first drift, or so you think. But, look what happens — the boat drifts to point D, which is a considerable distance from point B. This is because the drifts weren't started in the same position. Remember, fluke will often congregate in a very narrow zone and a drift that misses them by as little as ten feet can be fruitless. Without a reference point, it's easy to see why the angler can have difficulty making identical drifts when he is relying on visual observation.

The marker buoy gives the angler a reference point. It can be employed effectively in two ways. The first method is shown in Figure 3, where the buoy is dropped at point A, where the boat begins the drift. When the end of the drift is reached (point B) all the angler has to do is run the boat back to the buoy at point A to start a new drift. So long as the wind current directions haven't changed, the second drift will pass over the same area as the first, fulfilling the goal of the angler. This method should be employed when you are reasonably certain that the first drift will produce fish — otherwise you'll be wasting a lot of time putting out and pulling in the buoy.

At this point, many anglers make a serious mistake by bringing their fishing lines into the boat, starting up the motor and begin racing back to point A. Frankly, I don't know of many fluke caught when the lines and bait are lying on the floorboards of the boat, and the craft is creating a high rooster tail as it zooms at top speed towards the drift's original starting point. Rather than falling victim to this hurry-up approach, I'd suggest that you leave your baits in the water and begin a slow troll back to point A. Not only are your baits still in the water, but they will eventually pass over that productive spot you encountered during your drift. It's not unusual for someone to pick up as many fluke while trolling back to a starting location as they caught while drifting a productive stretch of bottom.

The second method of using a marker buoy should be employed when the productivity of a formation is unknown. In this case the buoy is dropped over the side when you have just hooked up with a fish. In the example we have been using, this is just as the boat passes through the rip, so the buoy is dropped as shown in Figure 4. Make sure the buoy is dropped as soon as the fish is hooked. *DON'T WAIT UNTIL THE FISH IS LANDED* to drop the buoy because the boat may have drifted a considerable distance during the interim. When the end of the drift is reached at point B, just move the boat

Marker buoys

In figures 3 and 4, it is usually more productive to troll from B to A after the drift.

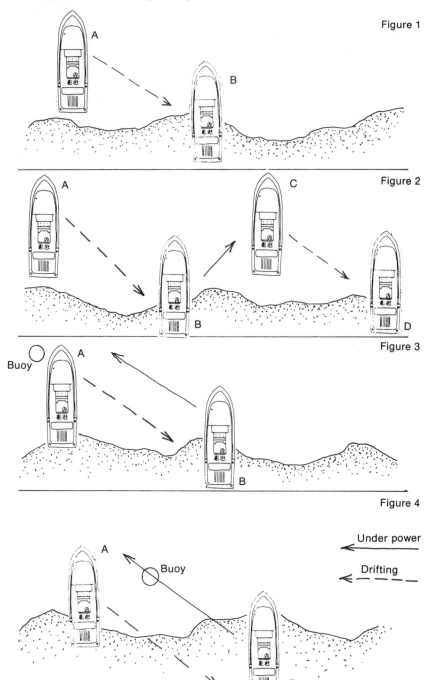

Figure 1

Figure 2

Figure 3

Buoy

Figure 4

Under power

Drifting

Buoy

99

in a straight line towards the buoy and *CONTINUE PAST THE BUOY IN A STRAIGHT LINE* until you are a sufficient distance from it to start another drift. The easiest way to be certain that you are moving in a straight line is with a compass. Before the boat is put under power to return for another drift, point the bow directly at the buoy and take a reading from the compass. Then just put the engine in gear and follow this course until you have passed the buoy and are in position to start a new drift.

As you can see, marker buoys can be an invaluable aid to successful fluke fishing so carry several in case one gets lost. Whenever possible, use a brightly-colored float that will be easy to spot on the water. Avoid white floats. If the water kicks up and there are white caps, a white marker buoy will become almost impossible to find. Wrap the line attached to the weight around the buoy so that it doesn't become tangled, and keep a buoy within reach at all times so that it may be thrown over at a moment's notice. Don't make the mistake of getting excited and dropping a buoy right on top of the fishing line, for obvious reasons. Throw the buoy either up-current or forward of the boat, where it won't tangle in any of the other lines in the water.

Ending a Drift

Where do you "end" a drift? I realize that I keep on saying things like "at the end of the drift" as if there was an "X" on the water at a precise spot that signals the angler to pull in his lines. There isn't any such "X marks the spot," naturally, so let's take a few lines at this point to discuss the length of a drift and when to terminate it.

In the example we have been using, a marker buoy has been dropped at the edge of a rip where a fluke was taken. After making a series of drifts and trolls taking several fluke, the angler will often discover that the fish are hitting during a very short time interval — which is just when the boat approaches and passes over the rip. It is extremely important that the angler recognizes this situation and knows what to do when it occurs. Let's see why, using the hypothetical situation presented in Figure 4.

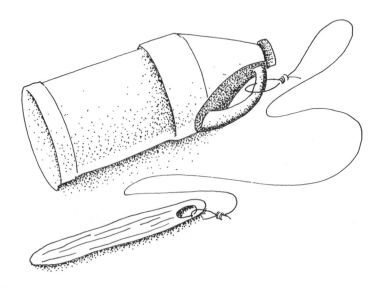

Let's assume that the first few drifts are made between points A and B, which is a distance of 1,000 yards and takes 10 minutes to traverse in the drifting boat. After several drifts, the pattern of fish on the rip line is observed. What do you do? Shorten the length of the drift to 500 yards, naturally. This cuts the drifting time in half, so in an hour's time you will be able to execute approximately 12 drifts instead of six. You will also drift over the feeding fish twice as many times, so you should double your catch. You aren't losing anything by shortening the drift — what you are doing is gaining the 2½ minutes at the beginning of the drift and 2½ minutes at the end that the other boats are wasting over unproductive bottom.

Lobster Pots

A lobster pot buoy is another stationary object that an angler may use as a reference point. Pots are also usually placed in areas where there are rocky shoals or reefs, the same types of bottom formation that often attract large fluke. The only problem is that a string of pots are often put out by lobstermen in numbers ranging from a half-dozen to 20 or more. To make matters worse, their buoys will often be the same color combinations and shape so that the owner can identify them as his own. So, if you do use a pot buoy as a reference point and aren't careful, you may be distracted and become confused as to which of them marked the hotspot you were fishing. They also cannot be used effectively to find an area on subsequent days because you will never know if and when the owner has moved them. Use lobster pots to locate the fish, but once the fluke have been found the best bet is to drop one of your own buoys over the side.

Navigation Aids

Navigational aids such as channel markers and buoys make excellent reference points for two reasons. First, they are more or less permanent and rarely removed, and they may be used for a reference point throughout the season with a large degree of confidence in their accuracy. Second, the very purpose of navigational aids is to alert boatmen to a condition that is potentially hazardous — the edge of a channel, a large shoal or rock, wreck, reef or sand bar, etc. These same conditions are often suitable for good fluke fishing. By consulting a nautical chart to find out what type of obstruction the navigational aid is marking, the angler may discover a bottom formation with good potential. If luck is with you and the spot turns out to be a good one, the navigational aid will serve as a reference point that can be used to find the hotspot on subsequent fluking expeditions.

And remember the motto suggested in Chapter Six: *Inshore of the buoys on Incoming — Offshore of the buoys on Outgoing.*

Shore Ranges

The only reliable method for finding hot offshore fishing areas and bottom formations accurately on a long-range basis is by the use of shore ranges. Marker buoys do the job when you are actually fishing, but it is impractical to leave a buoy to mark a hotspot and expect it to still be there when you return a week or more later. Shore ranges, however, are made with objects in fixed positions on land. Good ranges can be used over a period of years to locate a particularly productive area.

The principle of shore ranges is simple: two or more stationary objects on land will appear to be in different positions when viewed from different positions on the water. Put another way: by changing the position of a boat to the shoreline, stationary objects on land will be seen in different relative positions.

The best objects to use for taking ranges are those that are high and can be seen from a distance such as a water tower, tall building, telephone pole, radio tower, smokestack, antenna or a big tree. Large objects such as houses or buildings can also be used effectively. Large rocks right at the water's edge are excellent for taking ranges with an object set further back from the shoreline. Needless to say, never try to take a shore range with an object that isn't in permanent fixed position.

The accuracy of a shore range will increase in proportion to the distance between the two objects used, so it is important that the objects chosen for ranges are at varied depths from the viewer's eye. Chosing objects that are the same distance from the water's edge is almost worthless because as the boat's position on the water is changed their relative positions to each other will appear to have changed little. But when two objects are at different depths their relative position changes will be more pronounced.

Now, let's put the principles we have discussed into a practical application for fluke fishing. For taking our shore ranges we will use a hypothetical radar installation.

Four differenct shore ranges using the radar station are shown in the diagram. Let's suppose that you are in a boat drifting for fluke and hit into a pocket of fish on a good bottom formation. You want to take a range, so you look towards the shore and see that pole #3 is just touching the left side of ball B, as shown in Figure 1. Then you look at the depth recorder and note that you are in 54 feet of water. When the fishing dies and it's time to make another drift, you look up to see how the relative positions of pole #3 and ball B have changed, as shown in Figure 2. Pole #3 is now nudging the right side of ball B, pole #1 is at the left side and pole #2 is centered on the ball. This tells you that the boat has drifted from east to west. Now look at the depth recorder, which reads 60 feet, showing an offshore drift.

So, to make the same drift again, move the boat on a westerly inshore course until the range lines up as in Figure 1 and the depth rises 54 feet again. Then it's a good idea to continue in a straight line a little further, to a range observation as shown in Figure 3 or 4. This extra distance is to give the boat time to settle into the drifting pattern and you time to get the lines down before the boat drifts over the hotspot. If you stopped exactly on the position where the fluke were caught and the range was taken, the boat would probably have drifted past it before you were ready to fish.

A shore range gives the angle from shore of the position being marked. If there is a gradual increase in depth as you move away from the shoreline, then depth can be used to measure the position's distance from the shore. By combining the angle and the distance, the position is marked where the two bisect each other. In other words, the position we have taken a shore range on will be found by following the angle of the range until it bisects (or crosses) the 54-foot depth line.

But, what happens when you don't have a depth recorder or the depth is fairly consistent — how can you determine the distance from the location from shore? This calls for taking a double range. Using the same principles outlined for taking a single shore range, take a second range on objects as far away as possible from those used for the first range. By using two ranges, you not only get the angle from a shore location as you do with a single range, but also the distance. A double range will always mark a location where the ranges bisect one another — called "triangulatin" or "taking a fix."

Once you have taken a shore range for a bottom formation that produced a good catch for you, draw a detailed picture of the range in your diary or log book so that it may be used to find the position again at a later date.

Shore ranges

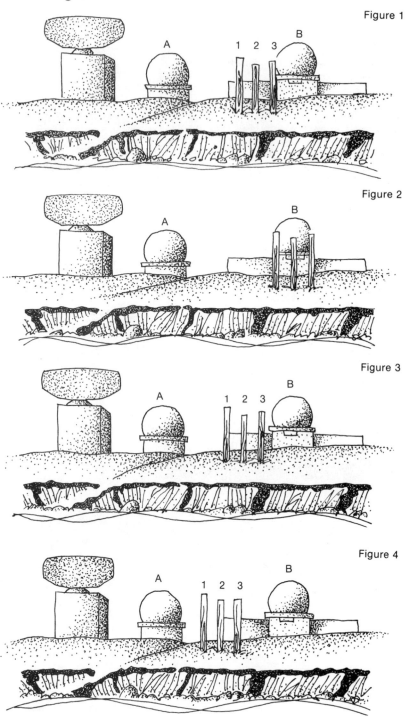

Figure 1

Figure 2

Figure 3

Figure 4

Compass Bearings

Compass bearings are a quick, accurate and simple method of plotting a position that you may wish to locate again. A bearing is simply a compass course between a boat and a fixed object on land. One bearing will give you the angle of the position from the object on shore, just as the single shore range will. Two bearings will give both the angle and distance from shore at the point where the bearings triangulate, just as the double range will. Three or more bearings will enable you to pinpoint the position even more accurately.

Taking compass bearings eliminates the necessity of drawing diagrams of ranges. In this case a few words can tell a lot more than pictures. The bearings "231° church steeple, 274° water tower, 326° lighthouse," entered into a diary or log book take the place of three diagrams showing three different shore ranges for triangulation.

Drift fishermen often find that the compass is just as helpful as the graph recorder and Loran in working a good pattern to catch a lot of fish.

Eric Burnley drifted the edge of a beach drop off casting a bucktail to fool this summer flounder.

Loran

For the past several years private and party boats have been using LORAN (**LO**ng **RA**nge **N**avigation) to find offshore fishing grounds. LORAN uses chains of transmitting stations, each having a master and several slave stations. These stations transmit a low frequency radio signal which the LORAN receiver on the boat interprets into the boat's location by translating the time difference between the signals from a pair of transmitting stations. The accuracy of most LORAN units to pinpoint a boat's location is within 50 feet and some of the newer units on the market claim that their accuracy level is within six feet.

If you already have one of these units onboard for blue water fishing, it can also be used to find offshore fluke-holding structure as well as finding inshore sites in bays when bad visibility makes the use of land markings impractical. If you've located a particular ocean or back bay hotspot for fluke and you want to return to this same spot the following day, just jot down in the log the numbers indicated on the LORAN unit which reflects your current location. Hopefully, the fluke will still be there. Some LORAN units even tell you that you need to steer the boat to the left or right in order to reach your selected destination point.

8
TROLLING
FOR FLUKE

While the most popular method of fishing for fluke is drifting, it is not always the most effective. When drifting, you tend to be at the mercy of the wind and tide and, in many instances, these two natural forces have pushed you over unproductive bottom structure. However, with trolling, you can position your boat over productive territory and, if the fluke are there, you'll outfish most of the surrounding boats that are drift-fishing. When you hear that certain fluke sharpies are putting together catches that are exceeding the century mark, you can bet that they know the bottom structure and layout of their areas and that they are probably trolling in order to give them the *BOAT CONTROL* they need to stay over the most productive spots.

Like every other style of fishing, there are certain do's and don'ts that make trolling a great way to catch many fish or leave you with alot of work and no fish. You must do it right to be successful.

As with drifting, the troller must run a series of patterns that take the boat back and forth over good bottom. Therefor, knowing where to troll is of paramount importance.

After figuring the right area to troll, the angler must then concentrate on the direction of the troll and the pattern of the troll. These two factors join together to make the boat swim past the fluke in a life-like manner.

Where to Troll

In Chapter Six, we described many types of bottom structures that hold fluke. Such areas as the lengths of channel edges, the down-tide edges of sand bars, the lengths of beach drop-offs, and the down-tide portions of a point of land are all excellent spots to use the trolling method instead of drifting. Notice how the previous sentence kept mentioning the words "length" and "down-tide." These two words are especially important as the areas described will hold the most fluke. The effective areas tend to be somewhat narrow and small. With such a size restriction, it's critical that you be able to position your boat where the fish are. There isn't too much room for error.

As a rule, when trolling with monofilament line, you will have to put a length of line out that is at least three times that of the water's depth in order to keep the rig on the bottom. So, the best depths to normally troll is water 10 - 15 feet deep, which means that you will only have to put out 30 - 45 feet of line. When fishing the flats, where you've found some minature bottom formations as mentioned in a previous chapter, only a few feet of line needs to be let out as the water is very shallow. Some talented fluke anglers that troll the skinny water of sand flats exclusively, claim that they catch the majority of their fish when their baits are almost in the prop-wash (and this is only in 4 - 5 feet of water), therefore, fluke are not motor-shy. Judging by some of the high scores these experts rack up, I wouldn't necessarily want to argue with them about the distance behind a boat that a bait should be trolled. As long as you can feel your sinker bouncing along the bottom, your bait should be in the fluke's feeding zone.

Direction of Troll

There tends to be some controversy between anglers that troll for fluke as to whether it's more effective to be trolling with the current or against it. Those that always troll with the current say that since most baitfish swim with the current, by trolling in this same manner, they present a more natural-looking bait. Those anglers that troll against the current imply that their technique provides a bait that appears to be struggling against the current and, since a fluke is a predator, these presentations make for easy pickings for hungry fluke. They also feel that if you are trolling with the current, your boat is probably going faster than the normal speed of the tide, because of the extra horsepower, making for an unnatural-looking bait.

I suspect that there is some truth in both of these arguments, so I'd like to suggest the following: Regardless of which way the tide is flowing, you should be more concerned with placing your boat over the most effective bottom formations. If a piece of bottom real estate is running east and west, and the tide is running north and south, you should be trolling the length of the structure as opposed to worrying about the direction of the tide. Often, there is a secondary channel edge branching off the main channel. If you were to either troll this secondary channel with or against the tide, you would pass over the most effective edges too fast. However, if you trolled cross-current of the tidal flow and worked the entire length of the branching channel edge, you would probably pick up more fish.

As a general rule, if the structure breaks are equal in direction with the tide and current flow, I'll tend to drift these areas with the current, and then troll back along the breaks with the current to my original starting point. In this manner, my baits are always in the water and, if I position my boat correctly, these same baits should be in productive territory.

If the tide and wind are working against each other, or if the structure breaks are not in the same direction as the tide, I will troll both up- and down-current, keeping the breaks in mind. There will be some days when most of the fish will be caught while going in one direction, and other days when it is just the opposite, so it pays to try both methods to see which is the most effective.

Trolling Speeds

The speed at which you troll the rigs is often very critical to success. What is the proper trolling speed for fluke? The answer may not sound too scientific and appear oversimplified, but the correct speed is the speed that catches fish. This speed can change in a few minutes' time, depending on wind and current conditions and the mood the fish are in. One minute it will be a crawl and the next minute three or four knots. So your best bet is to start trolling by moving the boat just fast enough to make progress over the bottom. If you make a pass without the bait getting any attention, troll at a slightly faster pace and continue to increase speed on each pass until you hook up with a fish. When the speed has increased to the point where the rig is planing off the bottom and a fish still hasn't been taken, move to another location and start over again.

If you have a high-powered, single outboard engine on your boat, you may experience a little difficulty trying to troll at the slower speeds. Some anglers overcome this problem by trolling backwards with the engine in reverse so that the stern of the boat moves first, slowing the trolling speed down considerably because of the increased water resistance.

I find it much easier to put the engine in gear and go until I am moving too fast, and throw it into neutral and coast. When the boat slows down, I throw the engine back into gear again and repeat the process. I have found this jolt-and-coast method of trolling for fluke very effective, particularly when fishing in deep water, where it is often difficult to keep the rig on the bottom constantly while trolling at any speed.

These trollers are working the edge of a shoal in hopes of making a good catch of summer flounder.

109

With my present boat, I can idle down my 35 hp motor to such a degree that I can just about crawl a bait along the bottom. The nice thing about this size engine is that when I tell my marine dealer to fill up the gas tank after a full day of trolling, the meter on the gas pump might show that only 3 - 5 gallons were needed to top off the tank. With inflation making fishing costlier, it's a nice feeling to only have to pay for a few gallons of gas at the end of a successful day of slow trolling.

Trolling Rigs

Each of the previously-mentioned rigs (one-hook, high-low and fish-finder) can be used effectively while trolling. However, in determining which rig is best to use, you have to consider the bottom formations you're fishing. For instance, if the bottom contains a lot of rocks, weeds, eel grass, etc., which makes spotting the bait difficult for a fluke, you should use the standard one-hook rig with a slight modification. Because of the length of line let out while trolling, and the ensuing loop scope, the distance between the end loop for the sinker and the first dropper loop for the hook end should be increased from 6 to 12 inches to a minimum of 18 to 24 inches. This will keep the bait a good foot to a foot-and-a-half off the bottom, where fluke will be able to spot the movement of your offering from a distance. Either a single hook or tandem hook arrangement may be used on the one-hook rig, depending on the choice of the bait being presented. Always use either a bank, ball or flat type sinker when trolling as they are less likely to become fouled on bottom obstructions. If you want to put more fish in the cooler, replace the bank sinker you're using with a sweetened bucktail of the same weight. Often, you'll catch double-headers with this simple trick.

However, if there is plenty of bottom debris in the area, you may want to use a three-way swivel where the normal first dropper loop is made on the line. To one eye of the swivel, attach your leader and hook; to another, attach your fishing line, and to the remaining eye, attach your sinker using a length of 18 - 24-inch line. The last length of line should be lighter in weight, so that if the sinker gets hung on the bottom, the lighter line will break, saving you the expense of an entire new rig.

If you are fishing bottom that is fairly smooth and sandy, the high-low rig is suggested. By using this dual-hook rig, you can place two baits in the fluke's feeding zone and, by moving the upper hook a little higher, you have a good chance of catching some other species such as weakfish or seabass. Those anglers that troll the sand flats effectively use the high-low rig exclusively as these fluke will be in small pockets. When such a pocket is found, these anglers want as many baits as possible trolling near the fluke in order to encourage double-headers.

There are days, however, when the fluke are biting lightly and you want to know when they pick up the bait. In this case, the fish-finder rig is a top trolling choice in that the fluke won't feel the weight of the sinker before you feel the drag of the fish. Only bottoms that are weed-free should be considered as the areas to be trolled with this rig, as the finder places your bait only an inch or two off the bottom.

Trolling Baits

Just about any of the standard fluke baits may be used for trolling, but I have found a few that seem to produce better than others. First off, live bait isn't necessary and doesn't even seem to have any advantages to speak of. The forward movement of the boat gives the bait all the movement it needs, so don't knock yourself out getting live bait and trying to keep it alive.

My favorite baits for trolling are killies or sand eels, which I rig in a somewhat unorthodox way. Instead of using just one, I place two or three baits on both the top and stinger-hook of a tandem hook. This gives the appearance of a small school of bait moving through the water that the fluke just can't resist.

My second preference for trolling bait is a thin strip bait that will have an enticing flutter as it is pulled through the water. The next time you fillet and skin a mess of fluke for the dinner table, save the skins from the white side and cut them into pennant shapes for trolling baits. Their thinness gives them a lot of flutter and they still have the smell that fluke love. The third choice for trolling is a 5- or 6-inch long, pennant-shaped strip of squid. Both the fluke and squid should be rigged on a tandem or Ryder hook.

Small boats with outboards are easy to steer with tiller extensions while trolling inshore waters and bay areas for fluke.

Trolling Patterns

There are three things to remember when establishing your trolling pattern. First, you want to position your boat over the 20% of the bottom that contains fluke. Secondly, you want to keep the boat over these productive spots as long as possible and, finally, you have to keep in mind where fluke position themselves during the various phases of the tide.

Let's talk about the last point. Normally, fluke will position themselves on the down-tide edge of any structure regardless of whether the tide is incoming or outgoing. The exception to this rule is during slack tide. The rationale for this down-tide positioning is that baitfish will be swept over the bottom with the current. As the tide passes over the piece of structure, water turbulence will be created, causing the smaller fish to become somewhat easy prey for the fluke that have set up a picket line along this edge. Therefore, it is along this down-tide edge that you must troll if you want to maximize your catch.

To place your boat over the most productive bottom structure for the longest period of time, you should know how this structure runs. Is it in a straight line, is it curved, does it come to a point, does it have a branching break? Knowing the outline of this structure, and in which direction it runs will help you position your boat. Sometimes a straight troll such as along channel edges is best, but when fishing along a beach's drop-off that is snake-like in contour, a zig-zag troll will put you over the best spots for a longer period of time. Finding how a bottom formation runs can be achieved in several ways. The easiest way is to be at your potential trolling spot during low tide. At this phase of the tide, many secrets of tidal flow and the causes of this flow should be revealed to you as many sections of the bottom will be visible. Using some of the higher structures along a coastline, such as buildings, cliffs, bridges, etc., will help you get a better idea as to how the local bottom is formed when these areas are viewed from these elevations.

Trolling Techniques

The actual trolling for fluke is relatively easy, since the boat does most of the work for you. However, you should be aware of several factors. First, and most important, you should let out a sufficient amount of line to keep the sinker bouncing along the bottom. If your sinker is two or three feet above the bottom, so is your bait, which takes it out of the fluke's feeding zone. The correct method is to let out line until the sinker touches bottom, then slowly feed out additional line until it makes at least a 60-degree angle with the water. The distance from rod to sinker will be approximately three times that of the water's depth. With the line angle of 60 degrees or more, the rig will always be on the bottom, unless the trolling speed is too fast.

Another thing to keep in mind when trolling is that often you will have to put your boat into tight turns to keep it positioned over a productive structure. When in this case, using longer rods such as those in the 7 - 7½-foot class is suggested as their extra length will help keep lines from becoming tangled. While some anglers mount their trolling rods in holders and then sit back to watch for a hit, I prefer to hold one rod in my right hand, as I'm steering the boat with the other.

There are several advantages to holding the rod: It allows you to feel when an additional length of line needs to be let out because the sinker isn't bouncing along the bottom any more, it allows you to instantly feel the fish mouthing the bait, and permits a quick drop-back, and it allows you to feel if your bait has become a victim of crabs, weeds, or other foreign matter.

You can tease a shy fluke into a second or, perhaps, third strike by pulling the bait away from him in short hops and then letting it settle back to the bottom. Finally, after many hours of trolling, you'll begin to develop an "educated right hand" that'll know what is happening to the trolled bait as it happens! No impersonal rod-holder can give you that kind of education, which, in the long run, will put more fluke in the box.

Trolling patterns — aerial view

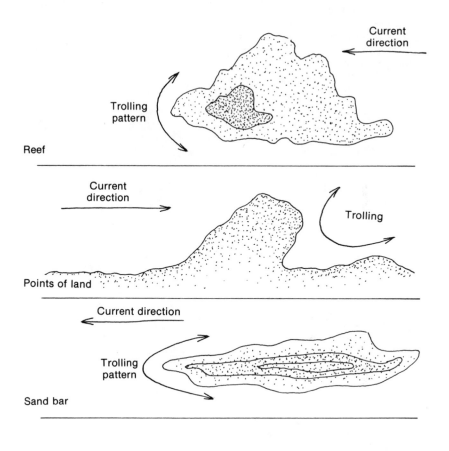

Current direction

Trolling pattern

Reef

Current direction

Trolling

Points of land

Current direction

Trolling pattern

Sand bar

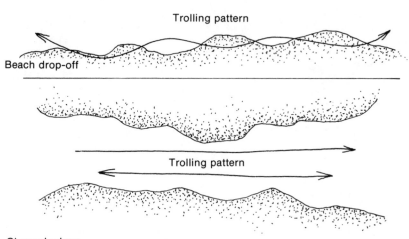

Trolling pattern

Beach drop-off

Trolling pattern

Channel edges

9
CHUMMING FOR FLUKE

Chumming is undoubtedly the most underrated of all techniques for taking fluke. In fact, very few anglers even know that it is a viable method of fluking. As a result, very little has been written on the subject, which is surprising because it works so well and the details should be shared.

When to Chum

Chumming for fluke is an extremely effective method when the fish are spread out over a wide area. This usually occurs when baitfish are relatively scarce, traveling individually or in small pods rather than thick schools. At these times the fluke are forced to leave the bottom formations, where feeding is easy work when food is plentiful, and must forage for food wherever they can find it. As a result, they are often scattered over wide areas of relatively flat bottom, which makes the job of locating fish in quantity very difficult for the angler. When this happens, drifting will usually only produce spotty results. The purpose of chumming is to gather these fluke together and lure them to the boat with the scent of an easy meal.

How to Chum

There are two basic methods of chumming for fluke, and both are employed while the boat is at anchor. Both methods accomplish the same result, which is to release tiny bits of food and odor into the current, where they will be carried a distance away from the boat. When a foraging fluke comes across the scent, he will turn and start swimming "upstream" to follow it to its source, eating the little tidbits along the way which serve to whet his appetite. Eventually, he will reach your boat and baited hook.

The first method of chumming works well in both shallow and deep water, but is particularly effective in depths of 10 feet and more. A frozen block of chum is placed in a wire-mesh chum pot or weighted plastic-mesh bag. The pot is attached to a strong line, lowered to the bottom and tied somewhere on the bow of the boat. As the warm water begins to defrost the frozen block of chum, it acts as a time capsule, releasing juices and tiny bits of meat into the current in a steady stream.

The second method of chumming works best in shallow bay waters, or may be combined effectively with the chum pot technique for fishing in intermediate depths. The chum is placed in a large bucket or can and mixed liberally with sea water to the consistency of a broth or soup. This concoction is then fed into the current in a steady stream with a soup ladle or small tin can nailed to a stick. Don't over-do-it, however — too much food in the water will allow the fluke to hang back and fill up on chum, instead of coming to the baits.

A variation of the soup method is to introduce small chunks of baitfish into the chum slick. It cannot be overstressed, however, that this technique can be counter-productive when over-done. Care should be taken to cut the baitfish into chunks no larger than an inch in length, and the pieces must be fed into the current sparingly lest the fish become overfed and lose the desire to follow the slick to its source.

Bunker Chum

Ground mossbunker (also know as menhaden) is probably the best all-around chum for fluke. It may be used in either a chum pot or as a soup mixture. Bunker chum is also readily available and is relatively inexpensive. The mossbunker is an extremely oily fish, which serves to make an excellent chum slick that will carry great distances before losing its luring effect.

Your best bet is to purchase bunker chum in the large 30-pound cans. These "tins" contain about three gallons of chum, which is usually enough for more than one fishing expedition for fluke. Purchase the chum frozen. If you are going to use a chum pot, chip a large frozen block of chum out of the can with a thick-bladed knife and place it in the pot or weighted chum bag and lower it to the bottom. To make a soup, place a block of the chum in a large bucket and add warm sea water and stir until it defrosts and breaks up. At the end of the day, take the leftover chum home with you. By this time it will have fully defrosted, so pour it into empty one-quart waxed milk containers and put them in the freezer. Then you have nice frozen blocks of chum for the next outing. Just cut off the waxed container with a knife and you're in business.

Baitfish Chum

Baitfish makes an excellent chum when they are cut into small pieces and fed into the current. This chunking method can be extremely effective at times, but there is always the danger of doing too much of a good thing and giving the fluke so much food to eat they never have to come close to the boat.

The problem with using baitfish for chum is the cost involved — they're just too expensive to use compared with bunker or squid chum. But the excess baitfish that are left over at the end of the day can be taken home and frozen. When enough frozen baitfish have been accumulated, take them on a fishing trip and use them for chum. Cut into chunks, they can be added to a chum slick to put a little meat in it, or the chunks can be fed into the current by themselves. Again, don't over-do it — drop a piece into the water, then wait until the current carries it out of sight before dropping the next chunk in.

Rigs and Techniques

The choice of rig that you use when chumming will be dictated by the depth of the water. When chumming on the flats of a bay where the water is six feet or less, the best rig to use is a float and a small splitshot. Attach the float to the line above a small beak hook approximately the same distance as the depth of the water. Then attach a small splitshot one or two feet above the hook. This will keep the bait just off the bottom within the feeding zone of the fluke, but it won't get snagged on the bottom or pick up seaweed.

The float rig is also extremely effective for live-lining small baitfish in the chum slick for fluke. Live bait is always preferable for bait when it is available, and the float will prevent the bait from hiding on the bottom. The split shot is just heavy enough to prevent the baitfish from staying near the surface, where the fluke are often reluctant to go, but not so heavy as to impede the baitfish's swimming abilities. Live bait choices for fluke are killies, small snappers, baby blowfish and grass shrimp. Take care to hook the baitfish lightly through the lips or in front of the dorsal fin so they will remain lively.

Using live bait and a float is also an excellent method of taking fluke from a pier, low bridge or a jetty. Get on the down-current side of the structure and allow the moving current to "walk" the float and bait away from your position. This allows the bait to cover a larger area in search of a hungry fluke, which is otherwise difficult when fishing from a stationary structure. The same chumming techniques may also be employed effectively here.

If live bait is not available when chumming, substitute with dead bait but make an effort to use the same bait as what you are chumming with. If you are chumming with bunker, put a chunk of bunker or a bunker heart on the hook; when using squid chum, bait up with a strip of squid, the head and tentacles or a whole small one; when chunking with spearing or sand eels, put two or three whole ones on the hook through the eye-sockets; if you have grass shrimp, place two or three on the hook, etc.

When using dead bait in shallow water, you can dispense with the float and just put the bait in the chum slick and feed out line so that the current carries it along with the chum. After the bait is about 150 feet away from the boat, reel in and repeat the procedure again. The same method is used when fishing with a float — let the current carry the float through the slick, retrieve and start over.

The chumming rig to use in deeper water is a standard one-hook rig, only the hook is attached higher up on the leader. By attaching the hook two or three feet above the sinker you will prevent the bait from dragging along the bottom where the fluke may not see it or it may pick up seaweed. The same baits are used as with the float rig, but there are two different methods of fishing the bottom rig. The first is to let the bottom rig out until sinker is about 25 feet behind the boat in the chum slick and just let it sit there, waiting for fluke swimming up the slick to find it. The second method is to "walk" the rig through the slick to bring the bait to the fish, which I consider most desirable and effective. To walk the rig, just lift the rod occassionally, then let out a few feet of line as the rig is lowered back to the bottom, which will move it a few feet further back in the slick. When the rig is far back in the edge of the chum slick, reel it in and start the "walking" procedure over again.

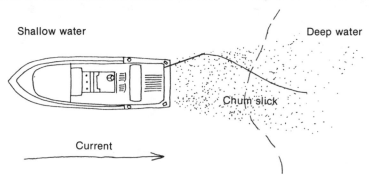

Shallow water   Deep water

Chum slick

Current

10
ARTIFICIALS FOR FLUKE

While drifting and trolling are the most popular and effective methods for catching fluke, using artificials is probably the most versatile and enjoyable way to catch them. Artificials can be cast from beachfronts, bulkheads, piers, jetties and boats with equal success. There are plenty of times when the wind and the tide conditions make it almost impossible to either drift or troll a bait, but casting from a boat that is anchored near a productive stretch of bottom structure in these adverse situations can often save the day with some outstanding catches of fluke.

It's amazing how one area of the coastline will see anglers using artificials such as bucktails, and yet you only have to travel some 50 miles to find another area where the fishermen are reluctant to try lures for fluke. What this second group of anglers fails to realize is that artificials will work if used properly ANYWHERE throughout the fluke's seasonal range. Rather than just dragging a bait along the bottom, as is the case when drifting or trolling, why not arm that casting or spinning rod with an artificial lure and have some fun. When you hook a fluke on an artificial, you tend to have a sense of accomplishment in that you've fooled the fluke into believing that your cast lure is actually something good to eat. With a throbbing rod tip and an angry fluke at the end of your fishing line, you can be proud of what you've achieved and that ear-to-ear grin is certainly in order. Does this type of fishing sound interesting and perhaps fun? Good, let's discuss how easy and effective it is to use artificials.

Bucktails

It's a safe bet to assume that at one time or another, most fluke anglers have tied on a bucktail, bounced it along the bottom a few times, caught little or no fish, and hurriedly stuffed this lure back into the tackle box to collect dust. Yet, in the hands of a bucktailing master this type of fishing format is truly an art form.

Before we go any further, let's clear up the definition of a bucktail, as some people call this lure a "jig" which, to another group, means a diamond-shaped lure that is used for bluefish. For our purposes, a bucktail is a lure that is molder out of lead. Included in the mold is a hook that rides in an upright position, to which is attached some type of hair for a tail. While most hooks on bucktails are solid, there are a few effective bucktails that have free-swinging hooks for more action.

There are basically four types of bucktail style lead-heads on the market. These include the Upperman (or flat), the Bullet, the Ball, and the Smilin' Bill (or notch face). Each of these heads have certain advantages, depending on the type of water being fished. For instance, the ball bucktail works best in back bays where the water is shallow, while the flat type is best in deep waters because it sinks faster.

Since bucktails come in a variety of weights, the water depth you're fishing will determine the weight to use. For waters under 5 feet, a ⅜-ounce bucktail is sufficient. If the depth is 5-10 feet, use a ⅝-ounce lure, and a ¾- to 1-ounce lure if the depth is over 10 feet. If you're working really deep water of 30-40 feet, a 2 - 3-ounce bucktail may be necessary. In my own case, I use a ⅝-ounce white bucktail in most of my bucktailing waters, which can range from 3 feet to 18 feet. I use the same weight because I've developed that "educated right hand" that knows instantly when there is something abnormal affecting the routine weight and action of the lure. If I were to keep changing lure weights I would have to become accustomed to these varied weights each time I switched lures.

By far, the most popular color of bucktail body is white with the same color hair attached to the hook. While some manufacturers have begun using synthetic hair because of its durability, the natural hair that comes off the tails of deer is still probably the best because of its breathing action. If the area has a supply of spearing as baitfish, you want to select bucktails that have a strip of silver mylar down the side, as this looks like a silvery spearing. The flash pays off.

Rather than using a snap or a swivel to attach your bucktail to the fishing line, tie this lure directly to the line using either a Palomar or clinch knot. This direct tie will allow you better control of the bucktail as well as providing for a faster hook-set.

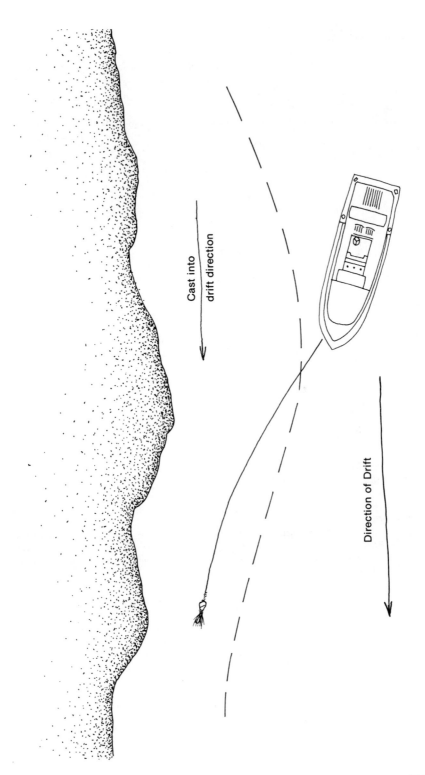

Cast into
drift direction

Direction of Drift

Now that you've selected your bucktail and have tied it on, you *MUST* sweeten the hook with some type of bait. Strips of squid, fluke belly, killies (hooked through the lips), sand eels and spearing all make excellent hook-sweeteners. When this type of lure and bait combination is used, the bucktail provides the weight and flash, while the bait provides the scent to draw the fluke to your hook. Never use just a plain bucktail for fluke unless you feel the need to just exercise your arm.

Bucktails work best in shallow water up to 12 feet in depth. These lures are extremely effective when cast to a beach drop-off, down-tide of a sand bar or along the edges of a depression or channel. When cast, they can be retrieved back to the boat or beach in several ways. However, the trick to bucktailing for fluke is to keep the lure as close to the bottom as possible. This can be accomplished by either retrieving the lure very slowly with 2 - 3-inch twitches of the rod tip or by retrieving it straight (again slowly) along the bottom. Those that whip their rod tips violently like working a popping plug for bluefish will soon become fishless victims with tired arms.

If casting is not your specialty, you can still use a bucktail effectively from a drifting boat. Just lower your bucktail to the bottom beneath your boat and begin a series of 2 - 3-inch high twitches of the top rod tip. The drifting boat will provide the forward motion for the lure, and slight up and down motion of the rod tip will impact action to the lure. This drifting technique is especially good when using multiple bucktails and rods.

A shad dart is a scaled-down version of a bucktail. These lightweight freshwater lures are very effective when fluking in shallow water (2 - 3 feet). I suspect that my two favorite colors for darts are gold (which resembles a calico crab), and green (which resembles a killie). Darts should not be fished bare but with a small piece of bait added. Since darts are very small (1/16 - 1/8 ounce), using line in the 4 - 6-pound class will provide better casting ability as well as improved line control.

Metal Lures

Metal lures such as the Hopkins and Ultimus are often very effective on a bright sunny day when there is good water clarity. The bright flashing of the metal seems to both attract the fluke and trigger their predatory instincts when they would otherwise be content to lie on the bottom. Metal lures are especially effective for fluke around jetties that contain sandy adjacent bottoms. The baitfish use the rocks of the jetty as a safe haven while fluke inhabit the surrounding sandy bottom waiting for a less than cautious baitfish to swim by. You should use metal lures that come with a single hook and bucktail hairs rather than a bare treble hook, and it's even a good idea to include a strip of squid on the hook as a teaser.

The Hopkins Shorty or Ultimus in weights of ¾ to 1 ounce are best for casting in shallow water up to 10 or 12 feet in depth. They may be cast downcurrent of a drifting boat and retrieved in one of three methods: a slow twitching action just off the bottom, a straight retrieve as slow as possible while still maintaining a side-to-side wobbling motion, or long sweeps of the rod followed by taking in the slack line that is created as the lure flutters and flashes as it sinks back to the bottom. When fishing in intermediate depths of 15 to 30 feet, lower a 1- to 3-ounce lure to the bottom and jig it by sharply raising the rod tip to a 45- or 60-degree angle, then lowering the tip so the lure flutters back to the bottom. Occasionally let out line to make sure the jig is still near the bottom within the feeding range of the fluke, which will usually strike as the jig is on its way back down to their position.

Diamond Jigs

A last resort when the fluke are lying in water 30 to 60 feet deep, where other artificials prove ineffective, is a diamond jig. Depending on the strength of the current and drifting speed, a 2- to 6-ounce diamond jig can be fished in the feeding zone of fluke in one of three methods: jigging, squidding or "walking."

Jigging and squidding with a diamond jig are both done while the boat is drifting. The jigging technique (as explained for the Hopkins) is most effective when fishing over a relatively flat bottom and constant depth where you can be reasonably certain of being in the feeding zone a large percentage of the time. But, when fishing over a rough bottom or formation where the depth varies greatly, squidding is more effective. Just lower the jig until you feel it bump bottom, then immediately make 5 or 10 turns of the reel handle so that the diamond jig darts upward at a moderate speed. Then lower it back down and keep repeating the process. An effective modification of a diamond jig is to replace the normal single hook with a Ryder hook. This solid tandem hook has a stinger in the rear, which allows you to use a combination of a jig and a strip of bait to tempt the resident fluke population.

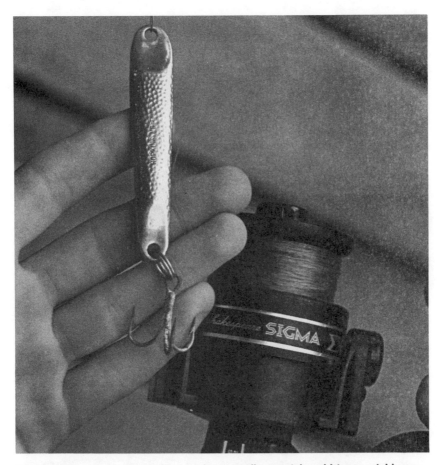

Surf fishermen and boaters often catch very well on metal squid-type metal lures.

11
HOOKING, LANDING & CLEANING

Our coverage of fluke fishing so far has concentrated on how to get the fish to take a bait or lure. We've discussed tricks and techniques. This last chapter will concentrate on how to hook the fish, bring it to the boat for landing, and, finally, how to clean your catch.

While inexperienced fishermen may believe in the "set the hook, haul 'em in" approach to fishing, there are techniques that will make your fluke fishing more productive. The so-called experts have developed ways of handling the tackle and manipulating the line to assure a higher hook up to strike ratio. Improperly working the rod to set the hook will actually lose alot of fluke for you rather than increasing your catch.

Handling the fish at boat side in the proper manner can also add to the day's catch; or decrease it. A generous sized net is a must have item, but is no guarantee that you'll boat the fish. This chapter will show the best way to lead the fish to the net, get him in the net and then bring him aboard for the cooler.

Small, undersized fluke should be released to grow larger and fight again on another day, but the release requires careful removal of the hook so the fish is not badly injured. Since many states have minimum size limits for the summer flounder, it's a good idea to have a mark on your rod handle or other handy place for a quick reference to easily judge if a fish is a throwback or a keeper. Many of the best fluke fishermen have established their own minimum sizes that are larger than the state's requirements. This spirit of conservation helps preserve the future of good fishing and enhances the sport value of the fish.

Certainly the summer flounder is one of the ocean's finest eating gamefish. With attention to the details of hooking your catch, playing it, netting the catch and finally getting it ready for the dinner table will pay off in some mighty fine dinners and lots of fishing pleasure.

The "Drop-Back"

One of the most difficult techniques to master in fluking is knowing when to set the hook. The key word is patience, patience, *PATIENCE*. Let's take a look at how the fluke will pick up a bait to see why patience is so critical.

When the fluke sees the bait slowly gliding along the bottom, it quickly intercepts and grabs it by the tail. But the bait continues to move as the boat drifts, confusing the fluke. He will then do one of two things: drop the bait, or swim along with it while trying to figure out what's going on. In either case, your reaction must be the same.

This is where the all important "drop-back" comes into play. When the fluke picks up the bait in the manner described, all that is felt by the angler is a nudge and a slight additional weight on the line, almost as if a piece of seaweed has been hooked. If the fluke elects to drop the bait, open the bail or put the reel into freespool and feed out 15 or 20 feet of slack line. This will give the fluke five or ten seconds to start swallowing the bait before the line straightens out with the boat's movement. If he is still hanging on, let him swim with the bait for at least 10 seconds before making the next move.

At this point, if you still feel the extra weight of the fish, point your rod to where the line enters the water. Then very slowly raise your rod tip to an angle of 45° and if the weight is still there, set the hook with a smooth lift of the wrist. This lift should drive the hook home into the fluke's mouth. Be sure that you've closed the bail on the spinning reel or engaged the handle. If you don't, you'll feel foolish holding a tangled mess of monofilament.

The important thing to avoid is striking prematurely, before the fluke has the hook in his mouth. If you strike and miss, the fulke will be spooked and rarely return. It is not uncommon to make four, five and even more drop-backs for a single fluke before he takes the hook and pulls back — and this is where novice flukers foul up. They get aggravated with this cat-and-mouse game, think "the heck with it" and strike too soon.

While striking prematurely is the cause of lost fluke, using dull hooks runs a close second in the "missed 'em" department. Even brand new hooks can arrive somewhat dull, so you can imagine the condition of a hook that has repeatedly hooked the bottom, debris, trash fish, gunnels and baits. After several fluke have been caught, I suggest that you use a few strokes of a Red Devil file to put a sharp, triangular point on the hook, and by all means, *NEVER* use the same hook from trip to trip no matter how lucky you think it is. Invariably it will lose you the biggest fish of the day — or perhaps the season!

Playing Your Catch

Unless you have hooked up with a fish in the doormat class, the actual playing of a fluke is easy — but there are a few do's and don'ts. For one thing, don't try to fight the fish with the reel . . . let him fight the bend of the rod — that's what a rod is for. When the fluke dives or takes line, don't keep reeling in — all you do is put a lot of twist in the monofilament without accomplishing anything. Most importantly, *NEVER* let the fluke have slack line to play with. If the hook hasn't been set well, a fluke can easily spit the hook with a shake of his head. So, make a point of keeping the line taut at all times.

If you hook up with a fluke of doormat size you're going to have a job on your hands just getting him to give up his suction-like hold on the bottom. You will feel very little evidence of life, just a tremendous weight as the doormat takes advantage of the volume of water pressing down on his flat body to stay on the bottom. All you can do is apply the maximum amount of pressure possible with the tackle being used. Take in all excess line, then slowly lift the rod so that it keeps bending until the drag starts to slip. Then just stop lifting and let the bend in the rod do all the work for you. Eventually the fluke will tire and give up his hold on the bottom.

Once he has, you must continue to apply pressure during the battle by "pumping" the rod to regain line. This is accomplished by first slowly raising the tip of the rod until it has a full bend at a 45-degree angle, then regaining line by reeling in as the rod is lowered to a horizontal position again. If the fluke dives and takes line, stop reeling — and make sure you don't give him any slack line.

Landing Your Catch

The last and most crucial part of catching a fluke comes when you're ready to land him. This can be a very tricky procedure for several reasons. As we have discussed, fluke will often be only lightly hooked in the lip or the flesh inside the mouth — as a result, many fish will be dropped in the water as they are lifted into the boat and the hook tears free. Fluke also have the annoying habit of playing possum when they are near the surface, remaining calm and stationary. This gives the angler a false sense of security as he may mistakenly believe the fish has been whipped and caught off guard when the fluke suddenly dives.

It's a virtual necessity to use a hand net to land a fluke that you want to keep. An all-around net for fluking should be at least 24 inches wide at the rim and have a deep pocket. A long handle is much preferred over a short one. If you have a small boat and storage space is a problem, purchase a net with a collapsible handle or put the net in a vertical rod holder for easy access. It's also advisable to have a net that will float in case it is accidentally dropped into the water.

A couple of "do's" and don'ts" that will save you more than a few botched up netting attempts . . . *DO* loosen your drag a bit before attempting to net a fish. When you have a lot of line out at the beginning of a battle, the fish

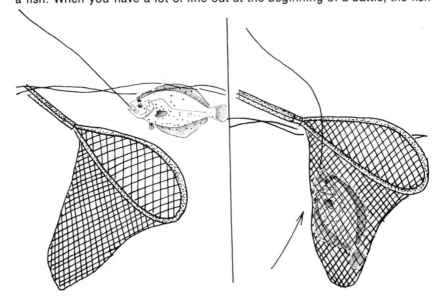

must fight a certain amount of elasticity in your line. When you are ready to net the fish, your line is very short and you lose this advantage. When the fish makes that inevitable last dive when he sees the net, you want to be sure he doesn't pop your line. Also, if the angle of the rod to fish is severe (causing greater friction between the line and rod), this will greatly increase the effect of the drag. If the fish surges, this drag can break your line or rod tip.

DON'T grab the leader! This oftens happens when a secondparty is doing the netting for you. By grabbing the leader you have given the fish something solid to pull against and he can quickly throw the hook. It can also badly cut your fingers (if the fish is large) or snap the leader.

There is only one way to net a fluke properly — head first. Always keep in mind that when a fluke is startled it will either swim forward with a short burst of speed or suddenly dive in an effort to reach the bottom. They will never, however, swim backwards into a waiting net, so approaching a fluke from the rear with a net is ridiculous, because as soon as he sees the net he will try to escape and he can swim through the water a heck of a lot faster then you can move a net to try and catch up with him. The trick is to position the net in the path of the escape so that the fluke will help to net himself.

Summer flounder have sharp teeth and care must be exercised to avoid injury while unhooking them.

Unhooking Your Catch

A fluke can be a dangerous fish to unhook, especially if caught on a tandem hook rig and there is an extra hook swinging about just waiting to sink into an angler's hand. The shape of their bodies makes them difficult to hold on to, and their relatively small mouths are powerful as well as full of many needle-sharp teeth. Fluke will be gut-hooked quite often, and have the annoying habit of just holding on to the bait as your reel them in without fighting much, so they come into the boat "green." A freshly-caught fluke can be difficult to unhook as the fish flips and flops on the deck. The fisherman should be careful to avoid the flying hooks as he attempts to grab the leader and then the fish.

If the fish is lightly skin-hooked, hold him up by the snell and shake until the hook tears out. If the hook is embedded firmly through the jaw, grasp the fish by putting the thumb of the left hand under one gill plate and the index finger in the other and squeeze. Put the point of a knife at the point where the hook is embedded, push it in about a half-inch, then twist the hook with the thumb and index finger of the right hand and free the hook with a twisting motion. If the hook is firmly lodged in the gills or at the back of the throat, use a hook-disgorger.

How To Fillet Fluke

While cleaning fluke is not perhaps the crowning event to an otherwise enjoyable fishing trip, it can be less of an arduous chore that many people make of this task. With the exception of the largest fluke, most fish can be filleted using just four knife cuts per side and, if done properly, these cuts should take you a total of 30 - 50 seconds per fluke, depending on your skill.

But before you begin to fillet your fluke, you should assemble some cleaning tools. First, I would make sure that I had a heavy cleaning board that won't slide around during the cleaning process. My own board measures 24 x 24 x 2 inches. It's a good idea to place a piece of high-pile indoor/outdoor carpeting on the filleting board to keep the fluke from slipping from side to side. Since I'm right-handed, I've borrowed a left-handed rubber glove from my wife's kitchen. This glove not only helps me to hold the fish in place on the board, but it also helps to avoid small knicks and cuts from a misplaced knife blade. Probably the most important item for easy filleting is a good quality steel, thin-bladed, super-sharp knife like one of the Normark Rapala line. The last item to be suggested for filleting is a metal fork, which helps with the skinning process (be sure not to use one from the matched silver pattern service for twelve).

Now for the cuts. With the fluke lying on the carpeted board, with its dark side up, make your first cut diagonally behind the head, making sure that the upper part of your cut includes most of the meat, and that the lower cut is below the entrail cavity. Make your second cut across the tail, but only down to the backbone. Slide your knife up the backbone and, by working the knife blade along the rib cage, make your third cut along the side fins. There is no need to make a special cut along the side fins as your blade will make this cut for you automatically as you work the rib cage. Make your fourth cut as you did the third, but in the other direction (from the backbone to the side fins). You should now have a fillet which can be skinned if desired. Repeat the preceding four cuts on the other side of the fluke to complete the filleting task.

The final step to filleting a fluke is the skinning process. Lay a fillet skin-down on the carpeted surface. Hold the narrow end of the fillet to the carpet with the metal fork. Cut down through the flesh and turn the blade of the knife flat against the skin with the sharp edge pointing towards the wide end of the fillet. Now start severing the skin from the flesh with a gentle sawing motion towards the wide end. Rinse the fillets lightly with fresh water and pat-dry with paper towels. The fillets can either be cooked now or placed in the freezer for later enjoyment. Freezing of fillets can be accomplished by placing them in double-wrapped freezer storage bags, or by freezing them in a block of water in an empty milk carton. Finally, save and freeze the skins for future use as strip baits.

1 — Make cut behind gill.

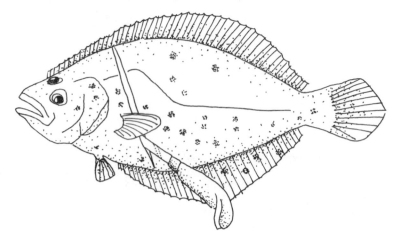

2 — Make cut at tail.

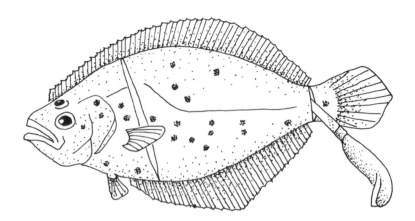

3 — Slide knife from tail to gill along back bone then swing handle to right.

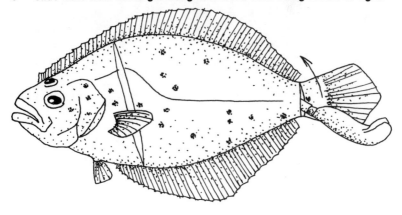

4 — Lift fillet to allow clean cut on left side.

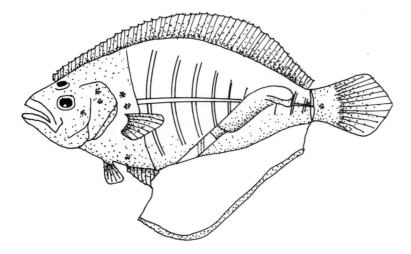

NOTES

NOTES

ABOUT THE AUTHOR

Don Kamienski can be classified as an angler who can put together excellent catches of fluke on a consistant basis, but he's always on the lookout for new and special techniques and locations for fluke. Don will use everything from aerial photographs to scuba gear to learn more about the habits of fluke. Each fishing trip provides some new information for him regarding the art-of-fluking that he'll file away for future reference.

This book describes many of the most effective techniques Don has assembled to win tournaments and party boat pools in over 25 years of fishing. By practicing the items recommended in this book, you'll be assured of a heavier cooler of fluke at the end of a day's fishing.

A graduate of Rutgers University, and a member of the New Jersey Outdoor Writers Association, his many articles have appeared in both regional and national magazines including THE FISHERMAN, N.J. Outdoors, N.J. Fishing Annual, Fins & Feathers, and Salt Water Sportsman. A frequent host and guest speaker at various workshops and sports expositions, Don takes his published fluke techniques and provides first hand demonstrations for hundreds of anglers annually. A tournament director on both the fresh and salt water scenes, his shared knowledge of various species has often helped the participants in the event.

When not writing, lecturing, field testing or directing tournaments, he can be found at the console of his boat, "Foggy Notion" on some quiet isolated stretch of water in pursuit of his favorite salt water specie . . . fluke.